NELSON
CENGAGE Learning

Financial
performance
Solvency
Financial
structure
Management
efficiency
Liquidity
Profitability

NCEA
Accounting
A NEXT STEP
LEVEL TWO

Analysis and Interpretation

Lilian Viitakangas with **Alastair Campbell**

ACCOUNTING A NEXT STEP Analysis and Interpretation
Student Book
NCEA Edition
Lilian Viitakangas
Alastair Campbell

Cover designer: Cheryl Smith, Macarn Design
Production controller: Siew Han Ong

Any URLs contained in this publication were checked for currency during the production process. Note, however, that the publisher cannot vouch for the ongoing currency of URLs.

For product information and technology assistance,
in Australia call **1300 790 853**;
in New Zealand call **0800 449 725**

For permission to use material from this text or product, please email **aust.permissions@cengage.com**

National Library of New Zealand Cataloguing-in-Publication Data
A catalogue record for this book is available from the National Library of New Zealand.

ISBN 978-017026-241-5

Cengage Learning Australia
Level 7, 80 Dorcas Street
South Melbourne, Victoria Australia 3205

Cengage Learning New Zealand
Unit 4B Rosedale Office Park
331 Rosedale Road, Albany, North Shore 0632, NZ

For learning solutions, visit **cengage.com.au**

Printed in China by RR Donnelley Asia Printing Solutions Limited.
1 2 3 4 5 6 7 19 18 17 16 15

Contents

Preface

Analysis and Interpretation is a stand-alone textbook/ workbook that has been designed specifically to cover Achievement Standard 91177 (2.4). It forms part of the *NCEA – Accounting a Next Step – Level Two* series, which has been developed to meet the requirements of the revised 2012 Level 2 Achievement Standards in accounting.

Acknowledgements

The authors gratefully acknowledge the assistance of those students and colleagues who have provided feedback on the earlier editions of this text and are especially grateful to Julie Green of Rosehill College for her invaluable feedback on this current edition.

Analysis and Interpretation

- Analysing the Income Statement
- More Profitability Measures
- Management Efficiency
- Analysing the Statement of Financial Position
- Writing a Report

Financial statement analysis is a technique that may be useful in evaluating the performance of a business in three major areas:
- Financial performance or earning capacity
- Management efficiency
- Financial position (liquidity, financial structure and stability).

Financial performance refers to the ability of the business to generate profits and to sustain them in the long run. Measures of financial performance are extracted from the income statement.

Management efficiency refers to the efficiency of management policies. The two most important as far as we are concerned are the credit collection policy and the inventory purchasing policy:
- Credit collection refers to the way the business goes about selling goods on credit, the checks that are carried out before a sale is completed, the terms of sale and the ability of the business to collect debts within a reasonable period of time.
- Inventory management policies are concerned with the amount and type of goods purchased and the timing of these purchases. It is important that the inventory does not run out, on the one hand, or sit around for a long period before sale on the other. Over-purchasing of inventory results in the increased risk of theft and the possibility that it may deteriorate or become out-of-date before it is sold. Excess inventory also ties up cash unnecessarily and results in higher warehousing and insurance expenses.

Financial position refers to the financial structure of a business, for example, the relative position of the owner in relation to the creditors of the business. It also refers to the ability of the business to meet its debts in the short and long term.

In earlier courses we met a number of commonly used ratios and percentages. Here we will revise those, learn some new measures of profitability and management efficiency and investigate the relationships between ratios and percentages more closely.

Analysing the Income Statement
The income statement provides a measure of the financial performance of an accounting entity, as shown by the profit (or loss), in a reporting period.

Consider the following example:

Wiremu is the owner of *Best Price Warehouse*, which is a discount store offering products to other retailers and also to the public. Wiremu has just received *Best Price's* financial statements from the accountant. He is pleased that the decision he made to increase advertising has produced an increase in sales. However, he is very concerned that, despite this increase in sales, profit for the 2020 year has decreased. He has asked us to explain how this might have happened.

The income statement for Wiremu's business is shown below.

Best Price Warehouse
Income Statement for the year ended 31 March 2020

$ 2019		$	$	$
	Revenue			
910,000	Sales			1,220,000
10,000	*Less:* Sales returns			20,000
900,000	Net sales			1,200,000
675,000	*Less:* Cost of goods sold			918,000
225,000	Gross profit			282,000
	Less: Expenses			
	Distribution costs			
4,200	Advertising	15,000		
5,000	Depreciation on delivery van	5,000		
65,000	Sales salaries	80,000		
32,000	Travelling expenses	55,000		
106,200			155,000	
	Administrative expenses			
2,700	Accountancy fees	3,000		
8,100	Bad debts	7,500		
2,400	Depreciation on buildings	3,000		
9,000	Discount allowed	12,000		
7,300	Insurance	7,500		
15,000	Office wages	17,000		
4,600	Rates	5,000		
3,400	Website and communications	4,500		
52,500			59,500	
	Finance costs			
9,000	Interest		15,000	
167,700	Total expenses			229,500
$57,300	Profit for the year			**$52,500**

The first thing we could do to help answer Wiremu's question is to present the income statement in the form of a pie graph for each year. These pie graphs are shown on the next page.

We can see that the cost of goods sold has increased slightly as a proportion of sales from 2019 to 2020. Distribution and finance costs have both increased slightly while administrative expenses have decreased in proportion to sales.

ISBN: 9780170262415

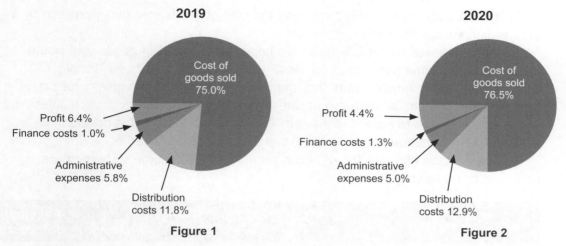

2019 | **2020**

Figure 1 | Figure 2

The result of these changes is that the profit has decreased as a percentage of sales by 2% – from 6.4% to 4.4%, even though the dollar figures for sales have increased.

In addition to looking at the proportion of each sales dollar consumed in meeting various expenses, it is also important to look at the figures themselves. Trends in the actual figures for various items are *just as important* as trends in percentage calculations.

Percentage Change

A useful guide to business performance may be found by looking at the percentage change in the various parts of the income statement between two reporting periods. For example, net sales increased from $900,000 in 2019 to $1,200,000 in 2020, which is an increase of $1,200,000 – 900,000 = $300,000. To calculate the percentage change, we express this difference as a percentage of the first year's sales:

$$\text{Percentage change in sales} = \frac{\$300,000}{\$900,000} \times \frac{100}{1}$$

$$= 33.3\%$$

This looks to be a *favourable* trend – the level of sales has increased in dollar terms. We would hope that this would lead to an increase in profit.

We can calculate the percentage change for all sections of the income statement. These calculations give us an indication of the trends in financial performance over the two-year period. We use the general formula:

$$\text{Percentage Change} = \frac{\text{This year's figure} - \text{Last year's figure}}{\text{Last year's figure}} \times \frac{100}{1}$$

For the cost of goods sold:

$$\text{Percentage change} = \frac{\$918,000 - 675,000}{\$675,000} \times \frac{100}{1}$$

$$= 36.0\%$$

Analysis and Interpretation

ISBN: 9780170262415

This is an *unfavourable* trend because the cost of goods sold has increased by a greater percentage than sales.

If sales increased by 33.3% we would hope that the cost of goods sold would increase by the same percentage (or less). Unfortunately, cost of goods sold increased by 36%, which means that the percentage increase in gross profit is *less* than the percentage increase in sales. The result is that less of each sales dollar was available to cover expenses in 2020 than in 2019. This conclusion reflects the information shown in the pie charts we prepared earlier.

The percentage changes for all of the sections of the income statement are shown in the following table:

Item	2019 $	2020 $	Change $	% change	Favourable/ Unfavourable
Net sales	900,000	1,200,000	300,000	33.3	F
Cost of goods sold	675,000	918,000	243,000	36.0	U
Gross profit	225,000	282,000	57,000	25.3	U
Distribution costs	106,200	155,000	48,800	46.0	U
Administrative expenses	52,500	59,500	7,000	13.3	F
Finance costs	9,000	15,000	6,000	66.7	U
Total expenses	167,700	229,500	61,800	36.9	U
Profit for the year	57,300	52,500	− 4,800	− 8.4	U

When deciding whether or not a trend is *favourable* or *unfavourable*, it is helpful to use the percentage change in sales as a benchmark. Remember that sales increased by 33.3%. If all the expenses also increased by 33.3%, then profit would increase by the same proportion and the outcome would be favourable.

We have already established that the 36.0 % change in cost of goods sold is *unfavourable* because it is more than 33.3%. If we examine the rest of the table, we find the following:

- **Distribution costs** have increased by 46%. This is an *unfavourable* trend because the increase is greater than the 33.3% increase in sales.
- **Administrative expenses** have increased by 13.3%. Since this is less than half the percentage increase in sales, the trend is *favourable*. It means that more sales have been achieved without a higher increase in the level of these expenses.
- **Finance costs** have increased by 66.7%. This is the twice the percentage increase in sales, so the trend looks to be most *unfavourable*.
- **Total expenses** have increased by 36.9%. This is an *unfavourable* trend because the increase is greater than the 33.3% increase in sales. The increases in both distribution and finance costs have more than offset the extra efficiencies in administrative expenses.
- **Profit for the year** shows a decrease of 8.4%. This is an *unfavourable* trend, especially since sales have increased.

What can we conclude?

The negative percentage change in profit *appears* to be due to an increase in cost of goods sold, together with poor control over both distribution costs and finance costs. We need to examine the expense sections of the income statement **in more detail** before we can identify areas of the business that require further investigation.

 PHOTOCOPYING PROHIBITED

ISBN: 9780170262415

Activities

1 The figures in the table below have been extracted from the income statement for *Convenient Office Supplies* for the past two years.

Item	2016 $	2017 $	Change $	% change	Favourable/ Unfavourable
Sales	450,000	600,000	150,000	33.3	F
Cost of goods sold	300,000	450,000			
Gross profit	150,000	150,000			
Distribution costs	22,500	36,000			
Administrative expenses	18,000	21,000			
Finance costs	13,500	18,000			
Total expenses	54,000	75,000			
Profit for the year	96,000	75,000			

a Complete the table given above. The first item has been done for you as an example.

b Answer the questions below, using your calculations as a reference.

b **i** Explain why there has been no change in the gross profit from 2016 to 2017.

_____

_____

_____

_____

ii Give one possible reason for the increase in **distribution costs**.

_____

_____

_____

_____

_____

_____

iii Give one possible reason for the increase in **finance costs**.

_____

_____

_____

_____

2 The table below shows a summary of the income statements of *Fabulous Flowers* for the years 2021 and 2022.

Fabulous Flowers

Item	2021 $	2022 $	Change $	% change
Sales	250,000	300,000		
Cost of goods sold	125,000	143,750		
Gross profit	125,000	156,250		
Distribution costs	25,000	37,500		
Administrative expenses	17,500	20,500		
Finance costs	12,500	16,000		
Total expenses	55,000	74,000		
Profit for the year	70,000	82,250		

DO THIS!

a Complete the table given above.
b Answer the questions below, using your calculations as a reference.

b i Explain the reasons for the percentage change in gross profit from 2021 to 2022.

_____

_____

_____

_____

ii Explain whether the percentage change in **administrative expenses** is *favourable* or *unfavourable* and why.

_____

_____

_____

_____

iii Give one possible reason why the percentage change in profit for the year may be considered *unfavourable*.

_____

_____

_____

_____

_____

iv Give one possible reason why the percentage change in profit for the year may be considered *favourable*.

_____

_____

_____

_____

_____

ISBN: 9780170262415

8

Examining Sales and Gross Profit

We have seen that net sales for *Best Price Warehouse* increased from $900,000 in 2019 to $1,200,000 in 2020 which was an increase of 33.3%. Cost of goods sold increased from $675,000 to $918,000 in the same period, which was an increase of 36.0%. The overall result was that gross profit increased by 25.3%, from $225,000 to $282,000.

For a trading organisation, the gross profit is extremely important because it must be sufficient to meet all of the business expenses and earn a profit, so that the owner receives a return from his or her capital investment. The gross profit percentage shows the percentage of each sales dollar that is available to meet expenses. It is calculated from the formula:

$$\text{Gross profit percentage} = \frac{\text{Gross profit}}{\text{Net sales}} \times \frac{100}{1}$$

The calculations for *Best Price Warehouse* are shown below.

Gross profit percentage

	2019	2020
	$= \dfrac{\$225,000}{\$900,000} \times \dfrac{100}{1}$	$= \dfrac{\$282,000}{\$1,200,000} \times \dfrac{100}{1}$
	= 25.0%	= 23.5%

The gross profit percentage has decreased from 25% in 2019 to 23.5% in 2020. This gives us the first clue to the reason for the reduction in the profit percentage for the 2020 year. There are several reasons why a change in the gross profit percentage may occur. Some of these are:

- A change in sales mix (the proportion of inventory sold with different levels of markup)
- Deliberate reduction of the markup and/or reducing prices of existing stock in the hope of increasing sales
- Inventory stolen during the year
- Errors in stocktaking at the end of the year.

A business may change the types of goods it sells and/or the relative amounts of different types of goods sold may change. We must remember that the gross profit percentage represents an *average* figure that is made up from different goods which have different markups.

Sometimes it is necessary to reduce prices to clear older inventory. Sometimes, in order to maintain market share in the face of competition, price increases from suppliers may not be passed on to customers or may be passed on without the addition of markup. All of these events lead to a reduction in the markup percentage, which in turn means that the gross profit percentage also decreases.

> **Remember!**
>
> The dollar *markup* is the amount added to the cost of goods to determine their selling price.

Inventory stolen during the year is not present during the end of year stocktake, so is presumed to have been sold. Since no income has been received from these items, the cost of goods sold will be higher in proportion to sales and the gross profit percentage will decrease.

If inventory is counted incorrectly during stocktaking, there will be an error in the gross profit and hence the gross profit percentage. Inventory omitted from the stocktake will cause the cost of goods sold to *increase* and hence the gross profit percentage to *decrease*. On the other hand, sometimes inventory is counted twice in the stocktaking process. This has the effect of overstating the closing inventory, which reduces the cost of goods sold, leading to an increase in the gross profit.

Although the perpetual inventory system reduces the chance of this type of stocktaking error, it is still very important to check stocktaking procedures and inventory measurement if any unexplained deviation occurs in the gross profit percentage.

The gross profit is, of course, closely related to markup. The dollar figure for the gross profit is actually the markup which has been added to the cost price of the goods to calculate their selling price. The markup percentage is calculated according to the following formula:

$$\text{Markup percentage} = \frac{\text{Gross profit}}{\text{Cost of goods sold}} \times \frac{100}{1}$$

The calculations for *Best Price Warehouse* are shown below.

	2019	2020
Markup percentage	$= \dfrac{\$225,000}{\$675,000} \times \dfrac{100}{1}$	$= \dfrac{\$282,000}{\$918,000} \times \dfrac{100}{1}$
	= 33.3%	= 30.7%

For *Best Price Warehouse*, the markup percentage was 33.3% in 2019 but has decreased to 30.7% in 2020. Wiremu had been concerned about competition in the market from cheap imported goods and decided last year to change his inventory and promote New Zealand-made products.

It would thus seem that the markup has dropped because Wiremu has decided to sell a different range of goods that had different levels of markup from what he had stocked previously. However, in dollar terms, the gross profit has improved by $57,000 in 2020 so it would seem that this strategy was successful.

This example illustrates the importance of examining the dollar figures alongside the percentages we calculate from the financial statements. At first glance, a fall in the gross profit and markup percentages may seem to be an unfavourable trend. However, if accompanied by an overall increase in the dollar amount of gross profit, they could merely reflect a deliberate change in business strategy that has proved to be successful.

ISBN: 9780170262415

Activities

1. The figures in the table below have been extracted from the income statements for *Super Stationery Supplies* for the past two years. The sales mix of the business has remained the same over the two-year period.

Item	2021	2022	Change $	% change
Sales	$540,000	$690,000		
Cost of goods sold	$450,000	$600,000		
Gross profit	$90,000	$90,000		
Gross profit percentage	16.7%			
Markup percentage	20.0%			

DO THIS!

a Complete the table given above.
b Answer the questions below, using your calculations and the information given above as a reference.

b i Describe the trends in sales, cost of goods sold and gross profit.

_____
_____
_____
_____
_____

ii Fully explain the reasons for the change in the gross profit and markup percentages.

_____
_____
_____
_____
_____
_____
_____
_____
_____
_____

2. **Ignore GST in this question.**

The table on the next page shows a summary of the income statements of *Bigger and Better Bathrooms* for the years 2022 and 2023. The business supplies and installs bathroom fittings. No inventory is carried because the bathroom fittings are ordered specifically for each job.

Bigger and Better Bathrooms applies a standard markup to all jobs. The average price charged per new bathroom is $12,500.

Item	2022	2023	Change $	% change
Sales	$450,000	$450,000		
Cost of goods sold	$225,000	$200,000		
Gross profit	$225,000	$250,000		
Gross profit percentage	50.0%			
Markup percentage	100.0%			

DO THIS!

a Complete the table given above.
b Answer the questions below, using your calculations and the information given above as a reference.

b Fully explain the reasons for the change in the gross profit percentage.

_____
_____
_____
_____
_____

c *Bigger and Better Bathrooms* is concerned about competition and has decided to reduce its average selling price by $500 in 2024. However, the manager wishes to ensure that the dollar amount of gross profit does not decrease. Costs are expected to remain the same.

i Calculate the number of jobs completed in 2023 and the average cost of each job.
Working

Number of jobs = _____   Cost of each job = $ _____

ii Calculate the expected gross profit for each job completed in 2024.
Working

Gross profit per job = $ _____

iii Calculate (to the nearest whole number) the number of extra jobs *Bigger and Better Bathrooms* would need to complete in 2024 to maintain the current dollar amount of gross profit.
Working

Number of additional jobs = _____

iv Calculate the new average markup percentage that would be applied in 2024.
Working

Markup percentage = _____ %

Accounting – A Next Step

ISBN: 9780170262415

Analysis of Expenses and Cost Behaviour

We have examined the trends in gross profit and markup for *Best Price Warehouse* and found that Wiremu has stocked a different range of goods in the past year. This accounted for the reduction in the gross profit percentage between 2019 and 2020 which, in turn, has had an effect on the profit for the year.

It is now necessary to examine the **expenses** for the two years to see what effect these have had on the profit. This will also indicate how well Wiremu has managed to keep expenses under control. Remember the following formulae?

$$\text{Distribution cost percentage} = \frac{\text{Distribution costs}}{\text{Net sales}} \times \frac{100}{1}$$

$$\text{Administrative expense percentage} = \frac{\text{Administrative expenses}}{\text{Net sales}} \times \frac{100}{1}$$

$$\text{Finance cost percentage} = \frac{\text{Finance costs}}{\text{Net sales}} \times \frac{100}{1}$$

These formulae are used to calculate the various expenses as a percentage of net sales. The sum of the individual expense percentages gives the total expense percentage, which can also be calculated directly from the following formula:

$$\text{Total expense percentage} = \frac{\text{Total expenses}}{\text{Net sales}} \times \frac{100}{1}$$

We will calculate these percentages for *Best Price Warehouse* later. It is not really possible to comment on the percentages for a particular business until we have some understanding of the way costs behave.

Consider the following example:

The table below shows the behaviour of two types of expenses, together with total expenses, with changes in sales volume.

Sales volume (000 units)	Expense A $	Cost per sales $ $	Expense B $	Cost per sales $ $	Total expenses $	Cost per sales $ $
100	40,000	0.40	20,000	0.20	60,000	0.60
200	40,000	0.20	40,000	0.20	80,000	0.40
300	40,000	0.13	60,000	0.20	100,000	0.33
400	40,000	0.10	80,000	0.20	120,000	0.30
500	40,000	0.08	100,000	0.20	140,000	0.28

If you examine the table, you will notice that Expense A does not vary, no matter what the sales volume. This type of expense is called a **fixed cost**. As sales volume increases, the cost per sales dollar decreases because the same amount of expense is spread over a larger number of sales dollars. Expense B, on the other hand, increases by an even amount with every sales dollar. This type of expense is known as a **variable cost**. The variable cost per sales dollar is constant because for every extra sales dollar, an additional unit of expense is incurred.

The total costs will therefore contain some fixed and some variable costs. Thus we expect the cost per unit to fall with an increase in the volume of sales. This is due to the effect of the fixed costs. As volume increases, the cost per unit decreases.

These ideas can be seen in graphical form below. Figure 3 shows the behaviour of *Expense A* with a changing volume of sales, while Figure 4 shows how *Expense A per sales dollar* varies with sales volume.

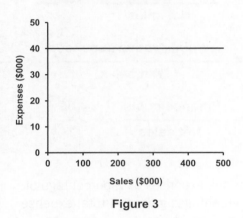

Expense A v Sales Volume

Figure 3

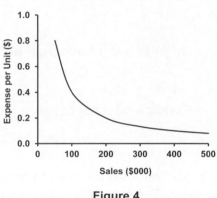

Expense A per Sales $ v Sales Volume

Figure 4

Figure 3 shows that the **total** Expense A remains *the same* across all sales volumes – a fixed cost. Figure 4 shows Expense A **per unit** *decreasing* as sales volume increases.

Figure 5 shows the behaviour of *Expense B* with a changing volume of sales, while Figure 6 shows how *Expense B per sales dollar* varies with sales volume.

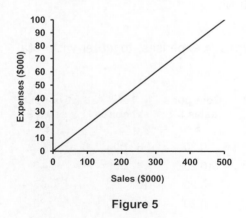

Expense B v Sales Volume

Figure 5

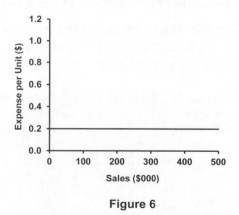

Expense B per Sales $ v Sales Volume

Figure 6

Figure 5 shows that the **total** Expense B *increases* directly in proportion to increases in sales volume – a variable cost. Figure 6 shows that Expense B **per unit** remains the *same* at all sales volumes.

Figure 7 shows the behaviour of *Total expenses* with a changing volume of sales, while Figure 8 shows how *Total expenses per sales dollar* varies with sales volume.

ISBN: 9780170262415

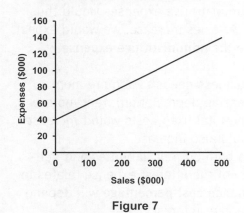

Total Expenses v Sales Volume

Figure 7

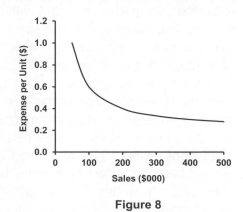

Total Expenses per Sales $ v Sales Volume

Figure 8

Total expenses consist of both fixed and variable items. Since there is a proportion of fixed costs, we would expect that total expenses per sales dollar would decrease as the volume of sales increases. This trend is shown in Figure 8.

Understanding how costs behave helps to analyse the efficiency with which operating expenses have been controlled in the business. Before drawing any conclusions about *Best Price Warehouse,* we will examine the different types of expenses normally incurred by trading organisations *in general*.

Distribution costs include items such as advertising, sales salaries or wages and delivery expenses. It would be reasonable to assume that as the sales of the business increase, these expenses would also tend to increase as we would probably need more sales staff and there would be increased costs for delivering the goods. These particular expenses are more likely to be of a variable rather than a fixed nature, and we would expect them to increase with sales. However, increased sales are often the result of an increase in the advertising budget. This may introduce an element of fixed costs because it is unlikely that sales vary directly in proportion to the amount spent on advertising.

On balance, it is likely that the distribution costs for a business will contain a higher proportion of variable costs than fixed costs. Thus as sales increase, we would expect the cost per dollar of sales to remain roughly the same. It may decrease slightly because in reality there will be a small proportion of fixed expenses such as depreciation on delivery vehicles. We thus expect the **distribution cost percentage** to decrease slightly with increasing sales, or at worst remain the same if sales increase. (If sales decrease, the percentage may *increase* slightly since the fixed expenses would be spread over fewer sales dollars.)

If the distribution costs *increase* as a percentage of sales, we should investigate the reasons for the increase. Deliberate decisions to increase the level of advertising, pay higher rates of sales commission or similar may be the cause of the increase and this would be perfectly acceptable. If sales have increased so much that more property, plant or equipment such as delivery vehicles were needed, the extra depreciation may also cause the percentage to increase. However, an increase in the distribution cost percentage could also mean that expenses have not been properly controlled. A close examination of each of the individual distribution costs is necessary to decide whether or not control over these expenses is adequate or not.

Administrative expenses include items such as rent, rates, insurance and depreciation, all of which tend to be fixed in nature over a particular range of sales. We would thus expect that as sales increase within this range, there

> **Remember!**
>
> If sales increase, the distribution cost percentage usually remains the same or decreases slightly.

Analysis and Interpretation

ISBN: 9780170262415

would not be a marked change in the total dollar amount of administrative expenses. The pattern of cost behaviour for administrative expenses would thus be most like Expense A in the example above. As sales increase, we would expect that the expense per dollar of sales (and hence the **administrative expense percentage**) would *decrease*.

If the sales volume rises so high that the business needs to acquire more property, plant or equipment assets (thus increasing depreciation), rent more space or increase other fixed expenses, then the total fixed costs would *increase* and the administrative expense percentage would also increase.

Finance costs consist of interest charges on both current liabilities and non-current liabilities. Most commonly, the majority of the interest expense relates to non-current liabilities. The behaviour of the **finance cost percentage** will depend on both the amount of debt and the trend in market interest rates.

If debt is being repaid steadily and interest rates remain constant, we would expect that, as sales increase, the finance cost percentage would decrease. If the finance cost percentage increases, the most common reasons would be:

- an increase in total borrowings, such as borrowing to purchase more property, plant and equipment; and/or
- an increase in market interest rates; and/or
- an increase in short-term debt (such as a bank overdraft), which usually attracts a higher rate of interest than long-term debt.

The table below summarises the expected behaviour of the different expense percentages as sales volume increases.

Class of expense	Expense type	Expected behaviour of expense percentage with increasing sales
Distribution costs	Mainly variable, with some fixed expenses	Remain constant or decrease slightly
Administrative expenses	Mainly fixed, with some variable expenses	Decrease
Finance costs	Mainly fixed, dependent upon debt levels and changes in market interest rates	Decrease unless borrowings increase or market interest rates increase

The expense percentages for *Best Price Warehouse* are as follows:

		2019	2020
	Total expense %	**18.6%**	**19.1%**
comprising:	Distribution cost %	11.8%	12.9%
	Administrative expense %	5.8%	5.0%
	Finance cost %	1.0%	1.3%

The distribution costs and finance costs have both increased as a percentage of sales, and therefore warrant investigation. The administrative expense percentage has decreased, thus it would appear to be satisfactory.

If we examine the income statement on page 4, we can see that Wiremu's expenditure on advertising has almost trebled in 2020. This was a deliberate decision made by Wiremu in an attempt to increase sales, which appears to have been successful. Sales salaries and travelling expenses have also increased, but

ISBN: 9780170262415

by a lesser proportion than sales in respect of 2019 levels. We can draw the conclusion that control over distribution costs has been reasonably good.

The statement of financial position shows that, in 2020, there was an increase of $60,000 in the mortgage and that Wiremu had taken out a new bank overdraft of $34,900. The interest rate on the mortgage has remained the same. These events explain why the finance cost percentage increased in 2020. However, we cannot draw any further conclusions until later in this module, when we will examine the financial structure of *Best Price Warehouse* in more detail.

Looking at Profit

The profit of a business for the year is calculated by deducting the total expenses from the gross profit. It represents the return to the *owner* from business operations.

The profit can be calculated as a percentage of sales to give a result commonly known as the profit percentage, according to the following formula:

$$\text{Profit percentage} = \frac{\text{Profit for the year}}{\text{Net sales}} \times \frac{100}{1}$$

The profit percentage is determined by two factors: the gross profit percentage and the total expense percentage. If the gross profit percentage decreases, then the profit percentage will follow unless there has been a corresponding decrease in the total expense percentage. If expenses increase as a percentage of sales, but there is no corresponding increase in the gross profit percentage, then the overall profit percentage will fall.

The calculation of the profit percentage for *Best Price Warehouse* is:

	2019	2020
Profit percentage	$= \dfrac{\$57,300}{\$900,000} \times \dfrac{100}{1}$	$= \dfrac{\$52,500}{\$1,200,000} \times \dfrac{100}{1}$
	$= 6.4\%$	$= 4.4\%$

The 2% decline in the profit percentage shows that *Best Price Warehouse* operated less efficiently in 2020 than in 2019. In the next section we will summarise the indicators of financial performance and try to establish reasons for the trends. So far, we have the following:

	2019	2020
Gross profit %	25.0%	23.5%
Markup %	33.3%	30.7%
Distribution cost %	11.8%	12.9%
Administrative expense %	5.8%	5.0%
Finance cost %	1.0%	1.3%
Total expense %	18.6%	19.1%
Profit%	6.4%	4.4%

ISBN: 9780170262415

Activities

1 The following table summarises the information contained in the past two years' income statements of *Kompact Outdoor Gardens*, which specialises in the design and manufacture of innovative garden furniture and planters for small city townhouses.

Kompact Outdoor Gardens

Item	2021 $	2022 $	Change $	% change
Sales	320,000	400,000		
Cost of goods sold	160,000	210,000		
Gross profit	160,000	190,000		
Distribution costs	36,000	44,000		
Administrative expenses	44,000	56,400		
Finance costs	20,800	24,200		
Total expenses	100,800	124,600		
Profit for the year	59,200	65,400		

Kompact Outdoor Gardens has researched its market and made some strategic changes in the past year. In particular, the markup has been reduced. Additional machinery was purchased to enable increased production. Office space was rented in the building next door so that the factory area could be extended into the old office space.

DO THIS!

a Complete the table given above.
b Calculate the percentages in the table provided below.
c Answer the questions below, using your calculations from **a** and **b** as a reference where relevant.

b Calculate the percentages in the table provided below.

	2021	2022	Working
Gross profit %	50.0		
Markup %	100.0		
Distribution cost %	11.3		
Administrative expense %	13.8		
Finance cost %	6.5		
Total expense %	31.5		
Profit%	18.5		

c **i** Describe the trend in administrative expenses and the administrative expense percentage over the two-year period.

_____

_____

_____

_____

Accounting – A Next Step

ISBN: 9780170262415

ii Identify the most likely reason for the change in administrative expenses, based on the strategy that *Kompact Outdoor Gardens* has employed in the past year.

_____

_____

_____

_____

iii Explain whether or not the owner of *Kompact Outdoor Gardens* should be concerned about the trend in the administrative expense percentage and why.

_____

_____

_____

_____

_____

_____

iv Explain the trend in finance costs and the finance cost percentage over the two-year period.

_____

_____

_____

_____

_____

_____

_____

v Identify the most likely reason/s for the change in finance costs, based on the strategy that *Kompact Outdoor Gardens* has employed in the past year.

_____

_____

_____

vi Identify the additional information you would require before you could establish the cause of the change in the finance cost percentage. You should state where you would find the information you would require and how you would use it.

_____

_____

_____

_____

_____

_____

_____

_____

Kompact
Outdoor
Gardens

vii Fully explain the reasons for the trend in the profit percentage.
Your answer should refer to any other relevant percentages.

_____
_____
_____
_____
_____
_____
_____
_____
_____
_____
_____
_____
_____
_____
_____

viii Explain whether or not the business owner should be concerned about the change in
the profit percentage and why.

_____
_____
_____
_____
_____
_____
_____
_____
_____

2 The following pie charts show the expense totals that have been extracted from the
income statements of *Competitive Imports* for 2023 and 2024. During 2024, the business
decided on an expansion strategy that was designed to increase profitability. The strategy
was based on increasing the product range, which in turn required leasing additional
warehouse space. A new assistant sales manager was employed. Existing cash reserves
were used to purchase new delivery vehicles, without the need for additional borrowing.

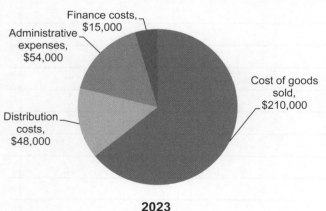

2023

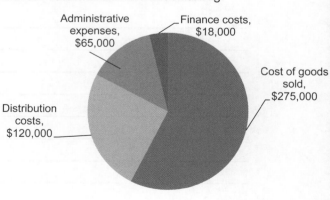

2024

🚫 PHOTOCOPYING PROHIBITED

ISBN: 9780170262415

DO THIS!

a Complete the table given below.
b Answer the questions below, using your calculations and the other given information as a reference.

a

	2023	2024	Working
Sales	450,000	575,000	
Gross profit	240,000		
Profit for the year	123,000		
Gross profit percentage	53.3%		
Distribution cost percentage	10.7%		
Administrative expense percentage	12.0%		
Finance cost percentage	3.3%		
Profit percentage	27.3%		

b i Describe the changes in sales, gross profit and profit for the year between 2023 and 2024.

_____

_____

_____

_____

   ii Identify the most likely reason for the change in the profit percentage.

_____

_____

_____

_____

_____

_____

   iii Suggest at least **three** specific reasons for the change in the distribution cost percentage.

_____

_____

_____

_____

_____

_____

_____

_____

_____

_____

_____

_____

PHOTOCOPYING PROHIBITED

Analysis and Interpretation

iv Identify the most likely reason for the change in finance costs between 2023 and 2024.

_____

_____

_____

v Give an opinion on the success or otherwise of the expansion strategy used by _Competitive Imports_ to improve profitability. In your answer you should comment on both **favourable** and **unfavourable** results of the strategy and suggest possible reasons for the 2024 profitability outcome.

_____

_____

_____

_____

_____

_____

_____

_____

_____

_____

_____

_____

vi Identify **two** aspects of the expansion strategy that the owner might investigate in order to improve the profitability of _Competitive Imports_ in the future and recommend changes that might be made. Justify each recommendation and explain:
- how your recommendation might improve profitability; and
- any risks involved with implementing the recommendation.

_____

_____

_____

_____

_____

_____

_____

_____

_____

_____

_____

_____

_____

_____

_____

ISBN: 9780170262415

More Profitability Measures

Profitability is essentially an efficiency measure that compares the profit for the year with some other aspect of business performance or structure. In the previous section, we measured profitability as the rate of return on sales of the business. However, there are two other measures of profitability that we must consider: **return on equity** and **return on total assets employed**. These two measures compare the profit with different aspects of the *financial structure* of the business.

Return on equity provides a measure of the return that the owner of the business has earned in return for *owning* the business. In other words, this means that it measures the return on the owner's capital investment.

There are two schools of thought regarding the best way to calculate this measure. The simplest formula is as follows:

$$\text{Return on equity percentage} = \frac{\text{Profit for the year}}{\text{Average equity}} \times \frac{100}{1}$$

In order to calculate the return on equity for *Best Price Warehouse*, we need information from the equity section of the statement of financial position. This information is shown below.

Best Price Warehouse

Statement of Financial Position (extract) as at 31 March 2020

2019 $		$
	EQUITY	
313,900	Opening capital	326,200
57,300	Profit for the year	52,500
(45,000)	Drawings	(50,000)
$326,200	Closing capital	$328,700

Average equity means the average of the opening and closing equity for the year. The calculations for *Best Price Warehouse* are shown below.

	2019		**2020**	
Return on equity percentage	$= \dfrac{\$57,300}{0.5*\$(313,900 + 326,200)} \times \dfrac{100}{1}$		$= \dfrac{\$52,500}{0.5*\$(326,200 + 328,700)} \times \dfrac{100}{1}$	
	= 17.9%		= 16.0%	

For *Best Price Warehouse*, the return on equity percentage was 17.9% in 2019 but has decreased to 16.0% in 2020. This has occurred for two reasons:
- the profit for the year decreased in 2020; and
- the average equity (capital employed) increased in 2020.

ISBN: 9780170262415 PHOTOCOPYING PROHIBITED **Analysis and Interpretation**

This is an *unfavourable* trend because Wiremu is now earning a lower return on his invested capital than previously so there is a *decreasing* trend in profitability.

If the owner of the business is also working in it, the formula we have used above can be misleading when the result is used to compare an investment of capital in a business with other forms of investment such as a term deposit in a bank. For example, the return of 16% on equity calculated above seems very favourable when it is compared to term deposit rates of around 5%.

When we consider the return on equity for a business, we are interested in what the owner is earning as a result of *investing* his or her capital. We must try and distinguish this 'owning' activity from the 'working' activity which is the actual running of the business.

As a result of the accounting entity concept, any amounts paid to the owner for his or her work in the business are considered to be *drawings*. Thus they are **not** expenses and therefore have no effect on the profit for the year. However, if a business owner decided to retire and pay someone else to do the work, wages would have to be paid to that person. Since wages **are** expenses, the profit for the year would *decrease* by this amount.

In a case like this where the owner had retired, the profit of the business would be the amount that a business owner earned just from **investing** in the business. Thus, to calculate a more accurate return on equity where the owner is actually working in the business, we should take the value of this work into account so we can measure the results of the investing activity **on its own**. We do this by deducting a notional (estimated) salary from the profit for the year in our calculations. Wiremu estimates that he would have to pay a salary of $40,000 to a manager.

The formula for this variation of return on equity is:

$$\text{Return on equity percentage} = \frac{\text{Profit for the year} - \text{'salary'}}{\text{Average equity}} \times \frac{100}{1}$$

The calculations for *Best Price Warehouse* are shown below.

	2019	2020
Return on equity percentage	$= \dfrac{\$57,300 - 40,000}{0.5*\$(313,900 + 326,200)} \times \dfrac{100}{1}$	$= \dfrac{\$52,500 - 40,000}{0.5*\$(326,200 + 328,700)} \times \dfrac{100}{1}$
	= 5.4%	= 3.8%

Assuming that the alternative term deposit investment has a return of 5%, the calculations show that the return on Wiremu's equity was comparable (or slightly better) than for a term deposit in 2019, but was less favourable in 2020. This is an *unfavourable* trend. Assuming that Wiremu could earn an annual salary of $40,000 elsewhere, he may be better off selling the business, investing his cash

ISBN: 9780170262415

in the bank and getting a job working for someone else. (This assumes that he could sell the business for a cash amount that is the same as his equity. He may or may not be able to do this, depending on how close the market value of the business assets is to their carrying amount in the statement of financial position. Another factor to be considered is the potential for goodwill to exist if this business is sold as a going concern. This would result in a higher selling price.)

When comparing the return on equity to returns from other forms of investment, it is also important to consider the amount of **risk** involved in each activity. Owning a business has a high level of risk, because the owner is personally liable for all business debts. If the business runs at a loss, then the owner's capital investment is eroded. On the other hand, a high level of profit can result in a business being far more rewarding in terms of returns than other investments. A term deposit is a relatively safe investment and has a low level of risk. It is highly unlikely that it would not be repaid at the end of the term and the returns are assured at a specified level.

A business owner should expect a higher level of return on equity than is available from alternative investments, to reflect the higher level of risk that he or she is taking by investing in the business. When these factors are considered, the return on Wiremu's investment in 2020 is even more unfavourable.

Return on total assets

While return on equity measures the efficiency with which the owner's capital has been used to generate profit, the return on total assets percentage measures profitability in terms of the efficiency with which **all the assets** of the business have been used to generate profit, regardless of how they have been financed. It answers the question: what is the return on all of the funds employed by this business? The formula is:

$$\text{Return on total assets percentage} = \frac{\text{Profit for the year} + \text{interest}}{\text{Average total assets}} \times \frac{100}{1}$$

Total assets of *Best Price Warehouse* for the past three years were:

Year	Total assets $
2018	510,000
2019	511,900
2020	698,800

The calculations are shown below.

	2019	2020
Return on total assets percentage =	$\dfrac{\$57,300 + 9,000}{0.5*\$(510,000 + 511,900)} \times \dfrac{100}{1}$	$\dfrac{\$52,500 + 15,000}{0.5*\$(511,900 + 698,800)} \times \dfrac{100}{1}$
	= 13.0%	= 11.2%

ISBN: 9780170262415 PHOTOCOPYING PROHIBITED **Analysis and Interpretation**

> **Note!**
>
> A return on total assets of 11.2% means that the business has earned 11.2 cents before finance costs for every dollar invested in assets, averaged over the past two years.

The calculation shows that the efficiency with which *Best Price Warehouse* has used its assets to earn profit has fallen from 13.0% to 11.2% between 2019 and 2020. This is an *unfavourable* trend. It means that *Best Price Warehouse* has not used the new assets as efficiently in 2020 as it had used its existing assets in the previous year.

Note that when the return on total assets percentage was calculated, the formula added back the interest expense to the profit for the year. This enables the efficiency with which assets have been employed to be measured *regardless of whether they have been financed by equity or by debt*.

The effect of the interest expense is to reduce the profit for the year. A business with more debt has a higher interest expense than a business with less debt. Using the profit amount *before* interest in the calculation enables more accurate comparisons between businesses with the *same* amount of total assets but *different* proportions of debt and equity.

We call the level of debt in relation to equity **gearing**. A business with a high proportion of debt compared to equity is said to be *highly geared*. If all other income and expense figures are the same, the profit for a highly-geared business is lower than for a business with lower gearing. If two businesses have the same total assets, but different levels of debt, their calculations for return on total assets would be different if we did not adjust for this interest expense.

A more highly-geared business would appear to be less efficient than one with a lower level of gearing, when in fact the efficiency with which total assets had been employed to earn profit was the same. Thus, failing to adjust for the interest expense would result in the wrong conclusion being drawn about the relative efficiency with which assets have been employed by the two businesses.

A summary of the return on investment measures is:

	2019	2020
Return on equity % (no salary)	17.9%	16.0%
Return on equity % (salary)	5.4%	3.8%
Return on total assets %	13.0%	11.2%

Since the profit percentage in relation to sales fell from 6.4% in 2019 to 4.4% in 2020, we would also expect the returns on equity and total assets to fall because the figures for both equity and total assets increased between 2019 and 2020. We discovered earlier that if term deposit rates are at around 5%, Wiremu might reconsider whether or not it is worthwhile for him to continue in business. The return on total assets, however, is well above the term deposit rate. If long-term borrowing rates are less than 11%, it could be worthwhile continuing since the return on the borrowed funds is higher than the cost of borrowing them.

So what should Wiremu do?

Some factors that Wiremu should take into account when deciding whether or not to continue in business are:

- His assessment of the likelihood that profits will improve in future. The expansion programme has been in place for a short time only. Increased advertising expenses partly account for the loss of profitability, but the benefits of this expenditure may well persist into future reporting periods.
- Wiremu may prefer to work for himself than find a job somewhere else, and be prepared to take the risk of investing his capital in order to do this.
- Market predictions relating to future interest rates and returns on alternative forms of investment.

  ISBN: 9780170262415

Activities

1 The information in the table below has been extracted from the financial statements of *Burly Productions*, which has a financial year ending on 30 June. The owner works full-time in the business, but is considering retirement. He has not yet investigated the cost of employing a full-time manager but will need to do this if he retires.

Item	2018	2019	2020
Profit for the year to 30 June	$100,000	$150,000	$200,000
Interest expense to 30 June (8%)	$20,000	$30,400	$30,400
Capital as at 30 June	$500,000	$520,000	$720,000
Total assets as at 30 June	$750,000	$900,000	$1,100,000

DO THIS!

a Complete the calculations in the table given below.
b Answer the questions, using your calculations and the information given as a reference.

a Complete the calculations in the table given below.

	2019	2020	Working
Total liabilities	$380,000		
Return on equity %	29.4		
Return on total assets %	21.9		

b **i** Explain why the interest expense remained unchanged between 2019 and 2020. Justify your reasoning.

_____

_____

_____

_____

ii Explain how *Burly Productions* has financed the increase in total assets that occurred between 2019 and 2020. Justify your reasoning.

_____

_____

_____

_____

_____

_____

_____

iii Comment on the trend in the **return on equity percentage** for the two-year period. You should state whether the trend is *favourable* or *unfavourable* and explain your reasoning.

_____

_____

_____

_____

_____

iv Comment on the trend in the **return on total assets percentage** for the two-year period. You should state whether the trend is *favourable* or *unfavourable* and explain your reasoning.

_____

_____

_____

_____

_____

When the owner of *Burly Productions* retires in 2021, he will need to employ a manager to run the business. He is concerned about the effect that this might have on profitability measures.

v Describe the effect of employing a manager on the profit for the year and explain your reasoning.

_____

_____

_____

_____

_____

_____

vi The owner will need to assess the performance of a new manager and plans on using measures of profitability to do this. Suggest a method that the owner could use to compare the profitability of *Burly Productions* before and after the manager is employed.

_____

_____

_____

_____

_____

_____

_____

Accounting – A Next Step

ISBN: 9780170262415

2 The information in the table below has been extracted from the financial statements of *Punaruku Fresh Produce*, a rural vegetable supply service, which has a financial year ending on 31 March. Miriama, the owner, works full-time as the local courier driver where she earns $50,000 per annum. She employs staff to run the vegetable supply business and also earns income from cash invested in term deposits at 5% per annum.

Item	2022	2023	2024
Profit before interest for the year to 31 March	$20,000	$25,000	$40,000
Interest expense to 31 March (8%)	$6,800	$5,600	$20,000
Capital as at 31 March	$290,000	$330,000	$350,000
Total assets as at 31 March	$375,000	$400,000	$600,000

DO THIS!

a Complete the calculations in the table given below.
b Answer the questions, using your calculations and the information given as a reference.

a Complete the calculations in the table given below.

	2023	2024	Working
Profit for the year	$19,400		
Total liabilities	$70,000		
Average equity	$310,000		
Average total assets	$387,500		
Return on equity %	6.3		
Return on total assets %	6.5		

b i Explain the reason for the change in the interest expense between 2023 and 2024.

_____

_____

_____

_____

_____

ii Describe the meaning of the return on equity of 6.3% that occurred in 2023.

_____

_____

_____

iii Describe the meaning of the return on total assets of 6.5% that occurred in 2023.

_____

_____

_____

_____

iv Explain the reason for the change in the return on equity percentage between 2023 and 2024.

_____

_____

_____

_____

_____

_____

_____

_____

_____

v Explain the reason for the change in the return on total assets percentage between 2023 and 2024.

_____

_____

_____

_____

_____

_____

_____

_____

_____

_____

_____

_____

vi Fully explain how the decision to purchase additional assets in 2024 has affected the **profitability** of _Punaruku Fresh Produce_ as measured by the following percentages:
- return on equity percentage
- return on total assets percentage.

_____

_____

_____

_____

_____

_____

_____

_____

_____

_____

_____

_____

_____

_____

ISBN: 9780170262415

vii Explain why the owner of *Punaruku Fresh Produce* should use **both** of the following return on investment measures to assess trends in the profitability of the business:
- return on equity percentage
- return on total assets percentage.

_____

_____

_____

_____

_____

_____

_____

_____

_____

_____

_____

_____

_____

_____

_____

_____

_____

_____

viii Using the measures of profitability calculated earlier, evaluate the profitability trends of *Punaruku Fresh Produce*. You should justify your conclusions with full explanations.

_____

_____

_____

_____

_____

_____

_____

_____

_____

_____

_____

_____

_____

ISBN: 9780170262415

Miriama has heard on the news that interest rates are likely to increase by at least 0.5% in the next year or so and is concerned that this may have an adverse effect on the profitability of *Punaruku Fresh Produce*.

ix Assuming that there are no other changes in the year to 31 March 2025, **fully** describe the effect that this increase in interest rates would have on

- profit for the year

_____

_____

_____

- return on equity percentage

_____

_____

_____

- return on total assets percentage

_____

_____

_____

Miriama is considering giving up her job as a courier driver to work full-time at *Punaruku Fresh Produce*. This would reduce business wages by $50,000 since she would cut back on current staffing and use this cash to pay herself.

x Assuming that there are no other changes in the year to 31 March 2025, **fully** describe the effect that this change in staffing would have on

- profit for the year

_____

_____

_____

- return on equity percentage

_____

_____

_____

xi Fully explain whether or not Miriama would be better off by cutting staffing and working in the business herself. Justify your answer with sound reasoning.

_____

_____

_____

_____

_____

_____

_____

_____

PHOTOCOPYING PROHIBITED

ISBN: 9780170262415

Management Efficiency

Management efficiency refers to the efficiency of management policies. In this course, we will consider two such policies: the inventory purchasing policy and the credit collection policy. We will calculate ratios that enable us to assess the efficiency of these policies and identify and analyse trends.

Inventory turnover

Inventory management is concerned with the amount and type of goods purchased and the timing of these purchases. The goal of efficient inventory management is to minimise the amount of cash that is invested in inventory. The following general principles apply:

- It is important that the inventory does not run out because this may result in customers buying goods elsewhere. Customers can be lost if a business develops a reputation for being out of stock.
- On the other hand, it is important that inventory does not sit around for a long period of time before it is sold. It may be damaged in storage, become obsolete or simply deteriorate with age. There is an increased risk of theft. Excess inventory ties up cash unnecessarily when it could be used for other purposes. It also increases warehouse storage and insurance costs.

Inventory turnover provides a measure of how often a business is selling its average stock in a reporting period (financial year). It is calculated from the formula:

$$\text{Inventory turnover} = \frac{\text{Cost of goods sold}}{\text{Average inventory}}$$

The result is expressed as *times per annum*. Inventory figures extracted from the statements of financial position of *Best Price Warehouse* for the past three years are as follows:

Year	Inventory $
2018	140,000
2019	160,000
2020	240,000

The calculations are shown below.

	2019	2020
Inventory turnover =	$\dfrac{\$675,000}{0.5*\$(140,000 + 160,000)}$	$\dfrac{\$918,000}{0.5*\$(160,000 + 240,000)}$
=	4.5 times per annum	4.6 times per annum

 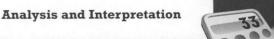

The calculations show that *Best Price Warehouse* sold the equivalent of its average inventory 4.5 times in 2019 and 4.6 times in 2020. The rate of turnover has thus remained approximately constant over the two-year period. It is not possible to say whether or not this rate is satisfactory as we do not know what the normal rate would be in this type of business activity. However, we can say that the increase in sales volume has not resulted in any loss of managerial efficiency as far as inventory management is concerned.

Different types of businesses have different rates of inventory turnover. Quite often those which have a low markup percentage, such as supermarkets, will have a fast rate of turnover while those with a high markup may have a lower rate. The rate for any particular business should be compared with others in the same industry to gauge the level of management efficiency. Comparisons of the same business from year to year will highlight changes in management performance. These comparisons measure how well managers are keeping up-to-date with what customers want in the current market:

- If the turnover slows down (fewer times per annum), there is the possibility that there is too much older inventory on hand and this should be investigated. In these circumstances, the business may be wise to reduce the selling price of any obsolete goods and obtain as much cash as possible for them.
- If the turnover speeds up (more times per annum), it may indicate that inventory management has become more efficient. However, too fast a turnover may also mean that the business is not holding enough inventory to meet customer demand, so this should also be investigated.

Age of accounts receivable (Accounts receivable turnover)

Age of accounts receivable (accounts receivable turnover) tells us the rate at which a business is collecting cash owed by credit customers. The formula is:

$$\text{Age of accounts receivable} = \frac{\text{Average accounts receivable}}{\text{Net credit sales} + \text{GST}} \times \frac{365}{1}$$

The age of accounts receivable may be expressed in a number of ways – often it is referred to as the *accounts receivable turnover, debtors' turnover, number of days' credit sales outstanding*, the *rate of collection of accounts receivable* or the *rate of collection of debtors*. The result is expressed as a **number of days**.

There are three important points to note about this formula:

- Only credit sales are used in the calculation, because cash sales do not result in an entry in the accounts receivable account.
- The formula uses **net** credit sales. This is because sales returns are removed from the accounts receivable account, so do not affect the rate of turnover.
- GST is *added back* to the figure for net credit sales that has been extracted from the income statement. This is because the income statement presents information on the GST *exclusive* basis, whilst the amount shown for accounts receivable in the statement of financial position *includes* GST. For the result to be meaningful and accurate, both the numerator and denominator of the formula must use figures that have been calculated on the same basis. (Note: It would also be possible to use an alternative formula that uses the income statement figure for net sales and deducts GST from the figure for average accounts receivable. The result of the calculation would be the same either way.)

ISBN: 9780170262415

Accounts receivable figures extracted from the statements of financial position of *Best Price Warehouse* for the past three years are as follows:

Year	Accounts receivable $
2018	92,000
2019	122,500
2020	225,000

The calculations are shown below.

	2019		**2020**	
Accounts receivable turnover	$= \dfrac{0.5 * \$(92{,}000 + 122{,}500)}{\$900{,}000 * 1.15}$	$\times \dfrac{365}{1}$	$= \dfrac{0.5 * \$(122{,}500 + 225{,}000)}{\$1{,}200{,}000 * 1.15}$	$\times \dfrac{365}{1}$
	= 38 days		= 46 days	

The calculations show that, in 2019, debtors were taking 38 days on average to pay their accounts. By 2020, this had lengthened to 46 days. This is an unfavourable trend, since *Best Price Warehouse* is taking longer to collect the cash that is owed.

Unlike other ratios, it **is** possible to have a 'rule of thumb' when discussing the age of accounts receivable of a business. Most businesses operate on normal credit terms – sales made to customers during a particular month are billed at the end of the month and are payable in full by the 20th day of the following month. This means that, on average, most accounts should be paid within 35 days of the sale. Consider the following:

Date of Sale	Date Billed	Due Date	Days Outstanding
1 March	31 March	20 April	51 days
31 March	31 March	20 April	20 days

The average of the number of days outstanding is approximately 35. If we allow that some customers may be a day or two late, we can say that a turnover of 35 to 40 days should be considered satisfactory for most businesses.

Some industries have different credit terms as the norm. For example, most firms in the retail computer industry demand payment within seven days. In these cases, the age of accounts receivable would be expected to be seven days. Thus we must adjust our expectations for the age of accounts receivable to suit the credit terms which are normal for the type of business under consideration.

In 2019, the age of accounts receivable for *Best Price Warehouse* was becoming unsatisfactory at 38 days and by 2020 it was an unacceptable 46 days. The reasons for this trend should be investigated. It is possible that Wiremu has become less efficient at collecting debts since the business has expanded and there are more debtors, hence more work in collecting cash owed. There may be some bad debts that have not yet been identified, which would have the overall effect of lengthening the turnover time. Another possibility is that Wiremu has offered extended credit terms as an incentive for customers to buy more goods.

> **Remember!**
>
> If there are bad debts in the accounts receivable ledger, the turnover time is longer.

  PHOTOCOPYING PROHIBITED **Analysis and Interpretation** 35

Activities

1 Calculate the inventory turnover for each of the scenarios **a** to **e** below.

	Inventory 31 March 2024 $	Inventory 31 March 2025 $	Cost of goods sold 31 March 2025 $	Inventory turnover (times per annum)	Working
a	30,000	30,000	150,000		
b	50,000	70,000	180,000		
c	43,000	47,000	225,000		
d	76,500	83,500	360,000		
e	26,500	53,500	100,000		

2 The information in the table below has been extracted from the financial statements of *Easyover Supplies*. The business has a financial year ending on 31 March.

Item	2022 $	2023 $	2024 $
Sales	100,000	120,000	120,000
Gross profit	20,000	30,000	20,000
Inventory as at 31 March	25,000	35,000	45,000

DO THIS!

a Calculate the following percentages for each year:
  i gross profit percentage
  ii markup percentage.
b Calculate the inventory turnover for 2023 and 2024.
c Describe the trends shown by your calculations and suggest reasons for the trends.

a

Year	Gross profit %	Working	Markup %	Working
2022				
2023				
2024				

b

Year	Inventory turnover	Working
2023		
2024		

c Describe the trends shown by your calculations and suggest reasons for the trends.

_____

_____

_____

_____

_____

_____

_____

ISBN: 9780170262415

_____

_____

_____

_____

3 Calculate the age of accounts receivable for each of the scenarios **a** to **e** below.

	Accounts receivable 30 June 2028 $	Accounts receivable 30 June 2029 $	Credit sales (including GST) 30 June 2029 $	Accounts receivable turnover (days)	Working
a	10,000	14,000	120,000		
b	50,000	60,000	300,000		
c	22,000	38,000	182,500		
d	56,500	63,500	730,000		
e	56,200	67,000	450,000		

4 The information in the table below has been extracted from the financial statements of *Wonderful Bargain Warehouse*. The business has a financial year ending on 30 June.

Item	2025 $	2026 $	2027 $
Credit sales	400,000	480,000	480,000
Accounts receivable as at 30 June	50,000	70,000	90,000

DO THIS!

a Calculate the age of accounts receivable for 2026 and 2027.

b Describe the trends shown by the data **and** your calculations and suggest a reason for these trends.

a

Year	Age of accounts receivable	Working
2026		
2027		

b Describe the trends shown by the data **and** your calculations and suggest a reason for these trends.

_____

_____

_____

_____

_____

_____

_____

_____

_____

Analysing the Statement of Financial Position

The statement of financial position of *Best Price Warehouse* is shown below.

BEST PRICE

Best Price Warehouse
Statement of Financial Position as at 31 March 2020

2019 $		$	$	$
	ASSETS			
	Current assets			
17,100	Cash at bank		—	
122,500	Accounts receivable (2018: $92,000)		225,000	
160,000	Inventory (2018: $140,000)		240,000	
2,000	Prepayments		1,500	
301,600	Total current assets			466,500
	Non-current assets			
210,300	Property, plant and equipment (Note 1)			232,300
511,900	Total assets			698,800
	Less: LIABILITIES			
	Current liabilities			
—	Bank overdraft (secured, limit $30,000)	34,900		
66,400	Accounts payable (2018: $51,000)	153,300		
3,000	Accrued expenses	5,550		
3,800	GST payable	3,850		
73,200	Total current liabilities		197,600	
	Non-current liabilities			
112,500	Mortgage (8%, due 31 March 2040)		172,500	
185,700	Total liabilities			370,100
$326,200	Net assets			$328,700
	EQUITY			
313,900	Opening capital			326,200
57,300	Profit for the year			52,500
(45,000)	Drawings			(50,000)
$326,200	Closing capital			$328,700

Notes to the statement of financial position

Note 1: Property, plant and equipment

	Land $	Buildings $	Delivery van $	Total $
For the year ended 31 March 2020				
Opening carrying amount	82,500	112,800	15,000	210,300
Plus: Additions	—	30,000	—	30,000
Less: Disposals	—	—	—	—
Less: Depreciation	—	(3,000)	(5,000)	(8,000)
Closing carrying amount	$82,500	$139,800	$10,000	$232,300
As at 31 March 2020				
Cost	82,500	150,000	25,000	257,500
Accumulated depreciation	—	(10,200)	(15,000)	(25,200)
Carrying amount	$82,500	$139,800	$10,000	$232,300

ISBN: 9780170262415

Looking at Liquidity

The term *liquidity* refers to the ability of a business to meet its debts in the short term. The significant factors in measuring liquidity are the current assets and current liabilities of the business. **Working capital** gives us a dollar measure of the excess of current assets over current liabilities – it gives an indication of the surplus of current assets for the next reporting period. It is calculated from the formula:

$$\text{Working capital} = \text{Current assets} - \text{Current liabilities}$$

It is impossible to specify an 'ideal' level of working capital – businesses of different types and different sizes have different working capital requirements. The current ratio (or working capital ratio) reduces the businesses to a common size and provides a better means of assessing the liquidity position in the short term. The ratio is given by the formula:

$$\text{Current ratio} = \frac{\text{Current assets}}{\text{Current liabilities}}$$

The current ratio measures the number of dollars of current assets which will be available to meet each dollar of current liabilities in the next reporting period. This should obviously exceed 1:1 or the business will not be able to meet its short-term debts. In businesses where a high level of inventory is held, the ratio may well have to exceed 2:1 to ensure a 'safe' level of cash will become available.

If the ratio is very high, there may be *too much* liquidity. Reasons for excess liquidity should be investigated. Common causes of a high current ratio are:

- the business may have excess cash which should be invested to earn income;
- there may also be too much inventory (too much has been purchased, or some of the inventory is obsolete); and
- there may be a high level of accounts receivable, due to poor credit control or bad debts that may be 'hiding' in the accounts receivable balance.

A high current ratio for any particular business may have arisen from any one or a combination of these factors.

The working capital for *Best Price Warehouse* is calculated as follows:

	2019	2020
Working capital	= $301,600 – 73,200	= $466,500 – 197,600
	= $228,400	= $268,900

In 2019 *Best Price Warehouse* had an excess of $228,400 of current assets with which to meet current liabilities and in 2020 this increased to $268,900. These figures indicate that the business should be able to meet its current liabilities due by the end of the next reporting period.

The current ratio is calculated as follows:

	2019	2020
Current ratio	$= \dfrac{\$301,600}{\$73,200}$	$= \dfrac{\$466,500}{\$197,600}$
	$= 4.12:1$	$= 2.36:1$

The calculations mean that *Best Price Warehouse* had $4.12 in current assets with which to meet each dollar of current liabilities in 2019 and $2.36 in 2020. At this stage the ratio looks satisfactory for both years, if perhaps a little on the high side in 2019. Indications are that the business should be able to meet its current liabilities by the end of the next reporting period.

We must remember that, although the current ratio can be a useful measure of liquidity, we should also examine the individual current assets and current liabilities in the statement of financial position before drawing any definite conclusions. In the statement of financial position of *Best Price Warehouse*, we can see that although the firm has a satisfactory working capital and current ratio, it has no cash. The bank balance has fallen from $17,100 in 2019 to an overdraft of $34,900 in 2020. The business has a bank overdraft limit of $30,000 and is over that limit by $4,900. The bank may demand repayment of this amount at any time, which could pose serious difficulties if *Best Price Warehouse* is unable to raise the cash.

More immediate measures of liquidity are shown by liquid capital and the liquid ratio (quick asset ratio, acid test). Liquid capital is given by the formula:

Liquid capital = Quick assets – Quick liabilities

where quick assets are those which we would expect to turn into cash *within the next month or so*. These include cash, accounts receivable and accrued income. We would **not** include inventory because, even if we sell it within a month, it is likely to turn into accounts receivable (for a credit sale) and it will be about two months before we collect the cash. We would **not** include any supplies on hand, for example cleaning supplies or stationery, because we intend to use those and they are not going to turn into cash at all. Nor would we include prepayments because these are expenses that have been paid in advance and will be used up by the business, not refunded.

Quick liabilities are those that must be paid in the next month. This includes accounts payable and accrued expenses and will normally include GST payable[1]. Income received in advance is not repaid in cash, so is **not** a quick liability.

---

1 For most small businesses, GST is payable to Inland Revenue when the GST return is filed every six months. If there is no GST payable in the month following the end of the reporting period, then GST payable would not be classified as a quick liability. However, most businesses organise their affairs so that the end of the GST taxable period coincides with the end of their reporting period, in which case the GST return is due in the following month and any GST payable **would** be a quick liability.

PHOTOCOPYING PROHIBITED

ISBN: 9780170262415

A bank overdraft is a quick liability only if it is 'on demand' or unsecured. An overdraft which is secured over the firm's assets is usually an ongoing arrangement with the bank and hence will not need to be repaid in the immediate future.

If an overdraft is over the limit set by the bank, then the *excess* must be considered a quick liability. (In practice, the bank would be most likely to contact a business about the level of overdraft before the annual accounts have been prepared. Unless temporary arrangements have been made, the bank is likely to dishonour payments if the business is over its overdraft limit.)

The liquid ratio is calculated as follows:

$$\text{Liquid ratio} = \frac{\text{Quick assets}}{\text{Quick liabilities}}$$

The liquid ratio measures the number of dollars of cash or equivalents (quick assets or liquid assets) that will be available to meet each dollar of current liabilities which are due for payment in the next month or so. This should obviously exceed 1:1 or the business will not be able to meet its *immediate* debts.

If we examine the statement of financial position of *Best Price Warehouse*, we can identify the following quick assets and liabilities:

	2019 $	2020 $
Quick assets		
Cash at bank	17,100	—
Accounts receivable	122,500	225,000
	$139,600	$225,000
Quick liabilities		
Bank overdraft (over limit)	—	4,900
Accounts payable	66,400	153,300
Accrued expenses	3,000	5,550
GST payable	3,800	3,850
	$73,200	$167,600

> **Remember!**
>
> Quick assets are sometimes known as *liquid* assets. They usually consist of current assets, less inventory and prepayments.

> **Remember!**
>
> Quick liabilities usually consist of current liabilities, less any secured bank overdraft and income received in advance.

The liquid capital and liquid ratio are calculated as follows:

	2019	2020
Liquid capital	= $139,600 − 73,200	= $225,000 − 167,600
	= $66,400	= $57,400
Liquid ratio	= $\dfrac{\$139,600}{\$73,200}$	= $\dfrac{\$225,000}{\$167,600}$
	= 1.91:1	= 1.34:1

The liquid capital calculations show that, at 31 March 2019, *Best Price Warehouse* expected a surplus of $66,400 cash after paying its immediate liabilities at the end of April. In 2020, this cash surplus was expected to be $57,400. The liquid ratio calculations show that in 2019, there was $1.91 of cash or equivalents to pay each dollar of immediate liabilities, due in April. In 2020 this amount was $1.34.

On first appearances, both of these calculations indicate that *Best Price Warehouse* should have no difficulty in meeting its immediate liabilities at the moment, but the downwards trend is disturbing. Take particular note of the amount shown for the bank overdraft. From the statement of financial position, we know that the bank overdraft is $34,900. Although the overdraft is secured against the assets of the business, it has a limit of $30,000. This means that the business is currently $4,900 over its limit and thus this amount should be considered to be repayable immediately. Since the overdraft is secured, the bank could seize other assets and sell them to meet this payment if *Best Price Warehouse* is unable to raise the cash. The excessive bank overdraft indicates that, despite the ratio indicators, there may be a cash shortage in the business. We will examine possible reasons for this in more detail in the next section.

A more commonly used version of the formula for the liquid ratio is:

$$\text{Liquid ratio} = \frac{\text{Current assets} - (\text{inventory} + \text{prepayments})}{\text{Current liabilities} - \text{secured bank overdraft}}$$

This formula gives the same result as the earlier formula, *provided that* the firm has no income received in advance. The calculations for *Best Price Warehouse* using this formula are:

	2019	2020
Liquid ratio	$= \dfrac{\$301,600 - (160,000 + 2,000)}{\$73,200}$	$= \dfrac{\$466,500 - (240,000 + 1,500)}{\$197,600 - 30,000}$
	$= \dfrac{\$139,600}{\$73,200}$	$= \dfrac{\$225,000}{\$167,600}$
	$= 1.91:1$	$= 1.34:1$

NOTE: Although used in examination resources, this formula is effectively a 'short-cut' formula which should be used with care. The most accurate way of calculating the liquid ratio is to examine the individual current assets and liabilities and assess which if these is likely to turn into cash, or be paid in cash, within the next month or so. Different businesses have different assets and liabilities and it is not possible to use a general formula such as this without some risk of including items that do not meet the criteria for quick assets or liabilities.

ISBN: 9780170262415

Activities

1 The information in the table below has been extracted from the financial statements of *Handy Hardware* for the past two years. The annual reporting period ends on 31 March.

	2027 $	2028 $
Current assets		
Cash at bank	1,500	—
Accounts receivable	18,500	20,000
Inventory	20,000	25,000
Current liabilities		
Bank overdraft (secured)	—	4,000
Accounts payable	18,000	23,000
GST payable	2,000	3,000

DO THIS!

a Calculate the current ratio for each year and explain the meaning of the ratios.
b Calculate the liquid ratio for each year and explain the meaning of the ratios.
c **i** Describe the trends shown by these calculations.
   ii Suggest possible reasons for these trends.
   iii Explain the consequences of the ratios you have calculated.

a Calculate the current ratio for each year.

2027	**2028**
Working	Working

ANSWER: Current ratio = _____ : 1 | ANSWER: Current ratio = _____ : 1

Explain the meaning of the ratios.

_____

_____

_____

_____

_____

_____

b Calculate the liquid ratio for each year.

2027	**2028**
Working	Working

ANSWER: Liquid ratio = _____ : 1 | ANSWER: Liquid ratio = _____ : 1

Explain the meaning of the ratios.

_____

_____

_____

_____

_____

_____

_____

c i Describe the trends shown by these calculations.

_____

_____

_____

_____

_____

ii Suggest possible reasons for these trends.

_____

_____

_____

_____

_____

_____

_____

_____

iii Explain the consequences of the ratios you have calculated.

_____

_____

_____

_____

_____

_____

_____

2 The information in the table on the next page has been extracted from the statements of financial position of *Fantastic Floorings* for the past three years.

DO THIS!

a Complete the calculations in the table provided.
b Explain the trends shown by the data given **and** your calculations.
c Suggest possible reasons for these trends.
d Describe the liquidity position of *Fantastic Floorings* at 31 March 2022 and make justified recommendations as to a course or courses of action the owner should take (if any).

Fantastic Floorings

Accounting – A Next Step

 PHOTOCOPYING PROHIBITED

ISBN: 9780170262415

Fantastic Floorings
Statement of Financial Position (extracts) as at 31 March

	2020 $	2021 $	2022 $
Assets			
Cash at bank	5,400	—	—
Accounts receivable	33,600	49,500	41,200
Inventory	40,600	56,500	59,500
Prepayments	1,400	2,000	2,300
Shop fittings	20,000	25,000	25,000
Equipment	5,000	7,000	25,000
Liabilities			
Bank overdraft (secured, limit $5,000)	—	3,500	7,500
Accounts payable	27,000	39,500	42,500
GST payable	1,000	2,000	2,500
Accrued expenses	2,000	3,500	4,000
Loan	10,000	15,000	15,000

a   Complete the table below. (Working space is provided beneath the table.)

	2020	2021	2022
Current assets			
Current liabilities			
Quick assets			
Quick liabilities			
Working capital			
Liquid capital			
Current ratio			
Liquid ratio			

Working

b Explain the trends shown by the data given **and** your calculations.

_____
_____
_____
_____
_____
_____
_____
_____
_____
_____
_____
_____
_____
_____
_____
_____
_____
_____
_____
_____
_____
_____
_____
_____

c Explain possible reasons for these trends.

_____
_____
_____
_____
_____
_____
_____
_____
_____
_____
_____
_____
_____

Accounting – A Next Step

 PHOTOCOPYING PROHIBITED

ISBN: 9780170262415

d Describe the liquidity position of *Fantastic Floorings* at 31 March 2022 and make justified recommendations as to a course or courses of action the owner should take (if any).

Analysis and Interpretation

Liquidity and Management Efficiency

In the previous section we were concerned with assessing the liquidity of a business – the ability of the business to meet its liabilities as they fall due in the short term. We used measures of working capital and the current ratio to assess the surplus of current assets over current liabilities in the next reporting period. We also used more immediate measures of liquidity in the forms of liquid capital and the liquid ratio to assess the amount of cash likely to be available to pay liabilities within the next month or so.

Ultimately, the majority of liabilities are paid in **cash**. (Income received in advance is the main exception.) The current and liquid ratios in themselves have limitations – for example they assume that all of the cash due from accounts receivable will be received. The liquid ratio assumes that this will occur within the next month.

It is more helpful to use a range of ratios when assessing liquidity. It is important to understand how cash flows through a business in order to interpret the measures of liquidity sensibly.

The cash cycle

The amount of working capital required by a business depends, among other factors, on the length of the **cash cycle**. This is the length of time between paying cash to suppliers and recovering it from customers. The cash cycle can be represented by the diagram below.

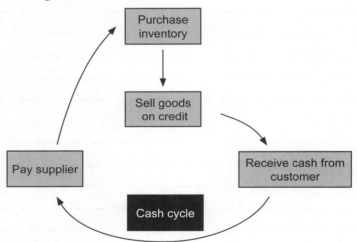

Ideally, a business would collect the cash from its customers before the suppliers need to be paid. This would minimise the amount of cash reserves required to be held, but is rarely the case unless a business has no credit sales. Under normal credit terms, suppliers require payment for goods, on average, 35 days after purchase. (This is the same period as we described under the age of accounts receivable section earlier.) The **accounts payable turnover** is the number of days between purchasing goods and paying suppliers. Unless the goods are sold on the same day as they are purchased, there will be a delay before the cash paid is recovered from customers. A time line of events is:

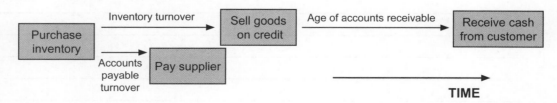

ISBN: 9780170262415

The **operating cycle** of a business is the length of time between purchasing goods from suppliers and receiving cash from customers. We can see from the diagram that this equals the number of days that inventory is on hand before it is sold plus the number of days before a customer pays the invoice. We can calculate the length of the operating cycle for *Best Price Warehouse* from the management efficiency ratios that we worked out earlier. First, however, we must calculate the number of days it takes to sell inventory.

Best Price Warehouse turned over its inventory 4.5 times in 2019 and 4.6 times in 2020. This means that in 2019, it took 365/4.5 = 81 days to sell the inventory and in 2020 it took 365/4.6 = 79 days. We can calculate the operating cycle for each of the two years as follows:

Year	Inventory turnover	Age of accounts receivable	Operating cycle
2019	81 days	38 days	119 days
2020	79 days	46 days	125 days

Thus the time between buying inventory and receiving cash from customers was 119 days in 2019 and 125 days in 2020. This is about four months.

The time between purchasing the inventory and paying the supplier in cash (accounts payable turnover) is, on average, 35 days. Thus *Best Price Warehouse* needed to finance the inventory for a period of (119 – 35) = 84 days in 2019 and (125 – 35) = 90 days in 2020. This is the length of the *cash cycle*, which is about three months. In other words, *Best Price Warehouse* is not collecting its cash from customers until three months *after* it has paid its suppliers for the goods. The long cash cycle may help to explain the large bank overdraft.

The longer the cash cycle, the higher the level of cash reserves that a business needs on hand if it is to meet its obligations on time. Extra cash is required to meet payments to suppliers while allowing for slow-moving inventory and/or longer than normal credit terms for customers.

Interrelationships between ratios

The above discussion illustrates the fact that the current and liquid ratios, on their own, do not provide an accurate picture of the liquidity position for a business. The liquidity of a business is also affected by its management efficiency – its ability to maintain a suitable inventory turnover rate and to control its accounts receivable. However, the current and liquid ratios **do** indicate areas of the business that should be investigated if there is a liquidity problem.

The table below provides a summary of the liquidity and management efficiency ratios of *Best Price Warehouse*:

Best Price Warehouse
Liquidity and Management Efficiency Summary

	2019	2020
Current ratio	4.12:1	2.36:1
Liquid ratio	1.91:1	1.34:1
Inventory turnover	4.5 times	4.6 times
Age of accounts receivable	38 days	46 days

Examination of the four ratios simultaneously gives a much clearer picture of what is happening in the business. The current ratio and liquid ratio both appear to be acceptable. However, the slow turnover of accounts receivable is an indication that the accounts receivable balances should be viewed with suspicion. If there is a high level of bad debts that should have been written off, then both current and liquid ratios would be artificially high due to the inflated figures for accounts receivable shown in the statement of financial position. Once the bad debts have been written off, both current and liquid ratios would be reduced and it is highly likely that the liquid ratio, in particular, would fall below 1:1. If this should prove to be the case, Wiremu would be unable to meet business debts that are due in the following month. The fact that the business has a bank overdraft that is over its agreed limit indicates that *Best Price Warehouse* is experiencing cash flow difficulties.

This example shows how the interrelationships between ratios are very important. Individual ratios *cannot* be considered in isolation because incorrect impressions may result. (Remember that both current and liquid ratios for *Best Price Warehouse* initially appeared satisfactory.)

We have established that a satisfactory or high figure for both the current and liquid ratios should lead us to investigate the age of accounts receivable. If we have a high current ratio and a low liquid ratio, we should immediately investigate the inventory turnover. This is because inventory is included in the current ratio but is omitted from the calculation of the liquid ratio.

The table on the opposite page provides some general guidelines as to areas which should be investigated when certain combinations of these ratios are found. You should note from the table that the level of bank overdraft also has a significant effect on both current and liquid ratios. The effect on the liquid ratio depends on whether or not the overdraft has been secured over assets of the business.

Even secured bank overdrafts are subject to review periodically and may be reduced or withdrawn. For this reason, it is more sensible to use short-term sources of finance to finance current assets such as inventory and accounts receivable and to use long-term finance to pay for property, plant and equipment. This is because property, plant and equipment are retained in the business for long periods, during which time they are used to generate income. This income can be used to pay the costs of financing (interest) and profits generated can be used to repay the debt. The recall of a short-term overdraft could result in the business being forced to sell its property, plant and equipment and thus being unable to operate.

'Window dressing' financial statements

We must also be aware that some businesses will *window dress* their accounts so as to give favourable impressions of liquidity and managerial efficiency in their statements of financial position. How often have you seen signs like these?

ISBN: 9780170262415

Investigating ratio interrelationships

Current ratio	Liquid ratio	Possible causes and areas to investigate	Possible action
High	High	Long age of accounts receivable which would inflate both ratios	• Write off bad debts and improve credit control procedures
		Too much cash on hand	• Invest surplus cash in interest-bearing deposits
High	Low	Slow inventory turnover, indicating overstocking or presence of obsolete inventory	• Check inventory and reduce the price of goods not in high demand • Write off obsolete inventory • Review purchasing procedures

Low	Low	Increase in unsecured overdraft	• Investigate potential sources of cash such as:
			  - collection of debts
			  - sale of obsolete inventory
			  - sale of excess property, plant and equipment
			  - additional contributions by the owner

		Check level of owner's drawings	• reduction of drawings
		Check means of financing property, plant and equipment	• Ensure that long-term assets have been financed from long-term sources and rearrange finance if necessary
Low	High	Large unsecured bank overdraft	• Ensure that long-term assets have been financed from long-term sources and rearrange finance if necessary

Such signs are very common just before the end of the reporting period. It is sensible for a business to reduce the level of inventory held before the end-of-year stocktake is held because the amount of work and the expense of carrying it out will be reduced if there is less inventory to process. However, the business may also have a 'hidden agenda' – a reduction in the level of inventory through having a sale will decrease the inventory shown in the statement of financial position and increase the level of cash on hand (or reduce the bank overdraft).

The figures shown in the statement of financial position in such a case will not be representative of the average levels throughout the year. The inventory turnover will look better that it really is (due to the lower level of inventory on hand at year-end) and the cash position will also be enhanced. Thus the statement of financial position may show a more favourable position than would be normal for the business. Before assessing a firm's creditworthiness, a potential creditor would be wise to investigate further than the annual financial statements (eg check with existing creditors or a credit rating agency).

ISBN: 9780170262415

 PHOTOCOPYING PROHIBITED

Analysis and Interpretation

Activities

1) The summary below shows analysis measures that have been calculated for three different manufacturers of packaged cakes that have a shelf life of six weeks.

Business	Current ratio	Liquid ratio	Inventory turnover	Age of accounts receivable
a	3.0:1	2.5:1	50 times	65 days
b	2.0:1	0.8:1	12 times	30 days
c	4.0:1	2.8:1	25 times	40 days

DO THIS!

Comment on the analysis measures given for each separate business. You should:
- explain whether or not each ratio appears to be satisfactory; and
- for each unsatisfactory measure, suggest areas of the business that require further investigation.

a _____

_____

_____

_____

_____

_____

_____

_____

_____

_____

_____

_____

_____

_____

_____

_____

b _____

_____

_____

_____

_____

_____

_____

_____

_____

_____

_____

_____

_____

_____

ISBN: 9780170262415

c _____

_____

_____

_____

_____

_____

_____

_____

_____

_____

_____

_____

_____

_____

_____

_____

_____

_____

_____

2 The following information has been extracted from the financial statements of *Disco Dan's Music* for the past three years. The annual reporting period ends on 30 June. Dan, the owner, is concerned about competition from on-line suppliers and wishes to monitor the trends in his business profitability, management efficiency and liquidity very closely.

	2022 $	2023 $	2024 $
Current assets			
Cash at bank	3,500	—	—
Accounts receivable	25,000	27,000	27,000
Inventory	40,000	44,000	60,000
Prepayments	1,500	1,000	3,500
	$70,000	$72,000	$90,500
Current liabilities			
Bank overdraft (secured, limit $5,000)	—	5,000	8,000
Accounts payable	20,500	23,000	23,500
GST payable	1,000	2,000	2,500
Accrued expenses	3,500	2,000	1,000
	$25,000	$32,000	$35,000
Other information			
Cash sales	100,000	150,000	155,000
Credit sales (net)	250,000	237,250	246,500
Cost of goods sold	210,000	252,000	260,000

DO THIS!

Answer the questions **a** to **e** below.

Working

a Complete the table below. (Working space is provided on the previous page.)

	2022	2023	2024
Quick assets	$28,500		
Quick liabilities	$25,000		
Gross profit	$140,000		
Gross profit percentage	40.0%		
Working capital	$45,000		
Liquid capital	$3,500		
Current ratio	2.80:1		
Liquid ratio	1.14:1		
Inventory turnover	6 times		
Age of accounts receivable	29 days		

b Explain the meaning of the following ratios at 30 June 2022:

i a current ratio of 2.80:1

_____

_____

_____

_____

_____

ii a liquid ratio of 1.14:1

_____

_____

_____

_____

_____

iii inventory turnover of 6 times

_____

_____

_____

_____

_____

iv age of accounts receivable of 29 days

_____

_____

_____

_____

_____

ISBN: 9780170262415

c For each of the following ratios and percentages, comment on the trend.
In your answers you should:
- explain the trend **and**
- give a possible reason for the trend, based on your calculations
  and the information given.

i gross profit percentage

_____
_____
_____
_____
_____
_____
_____

ii current ratio

_____
_____
_____
_____
_____
_____
_____
_____
_____
_____

iii liquid ratio

_____
_____
_____
_____
_____

iv age of accounts receivable

_____
_____
_____
_____

v inventory turnover

_____

_____

_____

_____

_____

_____

d Advise Dan whether or not the time taken by credit customers to pay their accounts is reasonable. Justify your reasoning.

_____

_____

_____

_____

_____

e Dan has received a letter from the bank manager, pointing out that the bank overdraft is over its agreed limit and demanding repayment of the excess within 30 days.

  i Explain the reason for the increase in the bank overdraft in 2024.

_____

_____

_____

_____

_____

_____

  ii Fully explain the probable consequences for _Disco Dan's Music_ if the excess bank overdraft is not repaid on time.

_____

_____

_____

_____

_____

_____

_____

_____

  iii Make a justified recommendation as to a course of action Dan could take to repay the excess overdraft and thus avoid these consequences.

_____

_____

_____

_____

_____

continued on next page

ISBN: 9780170262415

_____
_____
_____

iv Make a justified recommendation as to a course of action Dan could take to avoid this liquidity situation arising again in the future.

_____
_____
_____
_____
_____
_____

3 *Fresh Salads* buys fresh salad ingredients from the market and packages them for sale as convenience foods in local supermarkets. The following information was extracted from the statements of financial position as at 31 March 2024 and 2025:

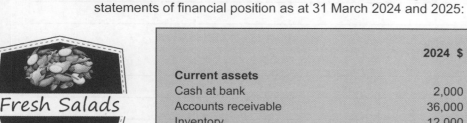

	2024 $	2025 $
Current assets		
Cash at bank	2,000	—
Accounts receivable	36,000	44,000
Inventory	12,000	16,000
	$50,000	$60,000
Current liabilities		
Bank overdraft (secured, limit $5,000)	—	20,000
Accounts payable	18,500	37,750
GST payable	1,500	2,250
	$20,000	$60,000

Additional information for the year ended 31 March 2025:
- Sales were $300,000 (excluding GST). Of these, 80% were credit sales.
- The gross profit was $160,000.

DO THIS!

Answer the questions **a** to **c** below.

a Complete the calculations in the table given below.

	2024	2025	Working
Current ratio	2.50:1		
Liquid ratio	1.90:1		
Age of accounts receivable	40 days		
Inventory turnover	15 times		

PHOTOCOPYING PROHIBITED **Analysis and Interpretation**

Fresh Salads

b   Explain whether each of the following ratios for **2025** is *satisfactory* or *unsatisfactory* and justify your choice.

i   Current ratio

_____
_____
_____
_____

ii   Liquid ratio

_____
_____
_____
_____
_____

iii   Age of accounts receivable

_____
_____
_____
_____
_____

iv   Inventory turnover

_____
_____
_____
_____

c   Explain **two** trends that have influenced the liquidity position of *Fresh Salads* in 2025. You should refer to both the data given and your calculations. Include in your answer:
   • a description of the trend in the liquidity position
   • an explanation of **two** possible reasons for this trend
   • a justified explanation of how each of these reasons has affected liquidity
   • justified recommendations as to any possible courses of action that *Fresh Salads* should take and how these would affect its liquidity position.

_____
_____
_____
_____
_____
_____
_____

continued on next page

Accounting – A Next Step   PHOTOCOPYING PROHIBITED   ISBN: 9780170262415

ISBN: 9780170262415

Analysis and Interpretation

Financial Structure

The term *financial structure* of a business is generally used to describe the relationship between debt (the amount owed to creditors of the business) and equity (the amount of the owner's investment in the business).

This can also be expressed by the equity ratio which shows the proportion of the total assets of the business that is financed by the business owner. The ratio is calculated from the formula:

$$\text{Equity ratio} = \frac{\text{Equity}}{\text{Total assets}}$$

This ratio should be at least 0.5:1. If the ratio is below this level, creditors have more of a financial interest in the business assets than the owner has. This may lead the business to experience pressure from creditors for payment. On the other hand, if the ratio is too high, the owner is not making use of all available external funds and could be limiting the expansion of the business by refusing to borrow.

Sometimes the equity ratio is interpreted as a measure of the level of confidence that creditors have in the business. A low ratio would mean that creditors are confident of repayment and are prepared to lend to the business at levels above normal. Conversely, a high ratio would mean that creditors have little confidence and are not prepared to lend.

It is difficult to specify an ideal value for the equity ratio. As with other ratios, it is important that the individual business be examined closely and the reasons for any trends identified. Comparison with industry averages is also a useful means of evaluating the ratios. The calculation of the equity ratio for *Best Price Warehouse* is shown below.

	2019	2020
Equity ratio	$= \dfrac{\$326,200}{\$511,900}$	$= \dfrac{\$328,700}{\$698,800}$
	$= 0.64:1$	$= 0.47:1$

The equity ratio has decreased from 0.64:1 in 2019 to 0.47:1 in 2020. This means that Wiremu financed 64% of the business assets in 2019 but this fell to 47% in 2020. The downwards trend is unsatisfactory, with the equity ratio now below 0.5:1. The result is that, in 2020, creditors of the business have a larger financial interest in the business assets than Wiremu. It is necessary to examine the statements of financial position carefully to try and discover the cause of this trend. If it continues, there is every chance that creditors could take control of the assets of *Best Price Warehouse*, particularly if the business has liquidity difficulties and creditors are not paid on time.

  ISBN: 9780170262415

We can see that Wiremu has withdrawn $50,000 in the year ended 31 March 2020. Since the profit for the year was $52,500, this means that only $2,500 was retained in the business for expansion. The mortgage has been increased by $60,000. This has been used to fund an increase in property, plant and equipment of $22,000, with the balance being used to increase the level of working capital. As we discovered earlier, the increase in length of the cash cycle (due to a longer age of accounts receivable), coupled with an increase in the level of inventory held, is the reason why more working capital was required.

Writing a Report

Analysis and interpretation of financial statements is carried out so that users of accounting reports may have better information with which to make decisions. The most important user of this information is the owner of a business. It is often the function of an accountant to prepare reports for owners and management that are based on ratio analysis. These reports explain the reasons behind results shown in the financial statements and advise on areas of improvement necessary for the successful future of the business.

An important principle in writing reports is *management by exception*. This means writing the report on the basis of the *unsatisfactory* aspects of the business performance so that the owner has information relevant to his or her needs.

The report on the following pages has been prepared for *Best Price Warehouse*. You should note the following points:

- Calculations are not shown in the report itself. Rather, a schedule of ratios and percentages is included as an appendix. This enables the report to be concise and free from extra material that the user may find distracting.

- The report has the following sections:
  - General comments
  - Financial performance
  - Management efficiency
  - Financial structure
  - Recommendations.

- The recommendations are listed together so that the owner can see immediately what action is necessary. This is clearer than incorporating them in the body of the discussion.

- The report is brief and to the point. Long discussion is not necessary. It must be remembered that owners and managers are busy people and do not wish to read through a rambling discussion that they may not understand. Any points needing further explanation can be covered at the personal interview, which normally follows the preparation of the report.

Wigglesworth and Topham

CHARTERED ACCOUNTANTS

P O Box 13-987   Newtown   Phone (08) 435-9654   Fax (08) 435-7342

email: service @wigtop.co.nz

Mr W Waenga
Best Price Warehouse
P 0 Box 15-756
NEWTOWN

1 July 2020

Dear Mr Waenga

Enclosed please find your completed accounts and supporting analysis.

General Comments

The expansion policy which you have put in place has not been successful
in improving the level of profit and has caused some difficulties that must be
addressed if your business is to survive in the short term.

Financial Performance

Although the level of sales has increased, the decision to reduce the markup
has had a detrimental effect on the profit for the year, which has fallen
by $4,800. The increase in distribution costs due to the heavy advertising
campaign and additional staff has also caused a reduction in profitability.
At the same time, there has been a considerable increase in the amount of
property, plant and equipment and the level of debt, due to the expansion of
the business. The net effect has been to reduce your return on equity to a level
far below that offered by banks for investment funds. The return on total assets
of 11.2% is still above the borrowing rate of 8%, which shows that the new
assets have been used effectively.

Management Efficiency

While inventory turnover has been maintained at a constant level, the rate of
collection of accounts receivable is an area of grave concern. Debtors are now
taking an average of 46 days to pay their accounts. You are financing these
customers through an expensive bank overdraft which has, in turn, increased
the level of interest payments and thus decreased the profit of the business.

Financial Structure

The financial structure of your business has become progressively weaker
during the year. The liquidity position is extremely serious as your bank

ISBN: 9780170262415

overdraft is well over its limit and it is likely that the bank could call it in at any time. At the same time the level of your equity has fallen from 64% to 47% of total assets which puts the business at increased risk from demands by creditors. The increased level of drawings has not been warranted and has caused the cash position to deteriorate.

Recommendations
1. If possible the markup should be increased. However this should only be done if the current quantity of goods sold can be maintained.
2. Tighter control over distribution costs is needed. The efficiency of the higher level of advertising must be measured and the increased level of travelling expenses should be investigated. Do the travelling expenses include any private travel which has not been recorded?
3. Credit policies must be tightened and accounts receivable investigated for the possibility of bad debts. Any bad debts should be written off.
4. The level of drawings must be reduced to preserve as much cash in the business as possible. A personal cash injection would help the liquidity position at present.

Please make an appointment to discuss these matters further at your earliest convenience. The preparation of your budget for the next year is of utmost urgency.

Yours faithfully

T G Wigglesworth

T G Wigglesworth
PARTNER

	2019	2020
Gross profit %	25.0%	23.5%
Markup %	33.3%	30.7%
Distribution cost %	11.8%	12.9%
Administrative expense %	5.8%	5.0%
Finance cost %	1.0%	1.3%
Total expense %	18.6%	19.1%
Profit %	6.4%	4.4%
Return on equity % (no salary)	17.9%	16.0%
Return on equity % (salary)	5.4%	3.8%
Return on total assets %	13.0%	11.2%
Inventory turnover	4.5 times	4.6 times
Age of accounts receivable	38 days	46 days
Current ratio	4.12:1	2.36:1
Liquid ratio	1.91:1	1.34:1
Equity ratio	0.64:1	0.47:1

Summary of ratios, percentages and interrelationships

When interpreting financial statements, it is tempting to focus on the calculated results and forget to examine these in conjunction with the source data in the financial statements themselves. To interpret trends in analysis measures accurately, it is essential to relate the calculations back to the detailed information in the financial statements, in order to draw reasonable conclusions and avoid making incorrect assumptions.

Consider the following example:

Energised Electronics is a supplier of computers, TV sets and other electronic equipment to businesses. The information below has been extracted from its financial statements for the years ended 30 June 2025 and 2026. The table also shows the percentage change for each item over the two-year period.

Item	2025 $	2026 $	% change
Income statement summary			
Net sales (all credit)	777,100	1,147,500	47.7
Cost of goods sold	405,300	568,700	40.3
Gross profit	371,800	578,800	55.7
Distribution costs	105,300	221,600	110.4
Administrative expenses	136,800	185,400	35.5
Finance costs	25,100	41,825	66.6
Total expenses	267,200	448,825	68.0
Profit for the year	104,600	129,975	24.3
Statement of financial position summary			
Accounts receivable	19,000	38,475	102.5
Inventory	25,000	75,000	200.0
Cash at bank (overdraft limit $25,000)	(28,000)	6,900	
Current assets	47,400	124,575	162.8
Accounts payable	21,500	25,200	17.2
Current liabilities	67,500	53,125	− 21.3
Property, plant and equipment	450,100	537,300	19.4
Total assets	497,500	661,875	33.0
Bank loan (8% per annum)	150,000	300,000	100.0
Equity	280,000	308,850	10.3
Drawings	100,000	101,125	1.1

The following notes are also available from the owner's diary:

2025 May 25	*Meeting with new suppliers to negotiate quantity discounts and inspect samples*
2025 July 14	*Remember to put ads for new sales staff on web site and in local paper*
2025 August 20	*New delivery vans due next week. Organise signwriting*
2025 September 19	*Advertise for extra office staff*

ISBN: 9780170262415

Examination of the raw data and percentage change calculations, together with the diary notes, enable us to identify the following trends before performing any further calculations:

- *Energised Electronics* has undergone an expansion programme during the year to 30 June 2026. This is evident from the 33% increase in total assets. The expansion has been financed by doubling the long-term bank loan and an increase of 10% in equity.
- Net sales have increased by 47.7%, but cost of goods sold has increased by a smaller amount (40.3%), which means that the increase in gross profit (55.7%) is higher than the increase in net sales. The diary note of 25 May indicates that *Energised Electronics* has changed its suppliers and negotiated quantity discounts. There may also have been a change in sales mix.
- Inventory on hand has increased threefold, even though cost of goods sold has increased by 40.3%. This may indicate overstocking. The accounts payable has only increased by 17.2%, meaning that the most of the increased inventory has been paid for in cash. This may be a result of the negotiations with the new supplier – perhaps discounts were received for cash payments and for buying goods in larger quantities than previously.
- Distribution costs have more than doubled, which indicates that there has probably been a deliberate increase in these expenses to try and increase sales. Sales wages have increased because more sales staff have been employed (diary note 14 July). New delivery vans have been purchased (diary note 20 August) which has resulted in higher depreciation charges and delivery van expenses.
- Administrative expenses have increased by slightly more than one-third. New office staff have been employed (diary note 19 September).
- Finance costs have increased by two-thirds. We would have expected them to double due to the doubling of the bank loan. However, the large bank overdraft has been repaid. Since the overdraft would have attracted a higher rate of interest than a long-term loan, there have been some savings of interest here.
- The overall result is that there has been an increase in the profit for the year of 24.3%, indicating that the expansion of the firm has been successful.

Profitability

The next step in the analysis is to calculate the percentages that enable us to assess the profitability of the business. A table summarising the formulae for these calculations and their meanings is shown on the next page. The table below summarises the profitability measures for *Energised Electronics*.

	2025	2026
Gross profit %	47.8	50.4
Markup %	91.7	101.8
Distribution cost %	13.5	19.3
Administrative expense %	17.6	16.2
Finance cost %	3.2	3.6
Total expense %	34.3	39.1
Profit %	13.5	11.3
Return on equity %	37.7	44.1
Return on total assets %	27.4	29.6

ISBN: 9780170262415 PHOTOCOPYING PROHIBITED **Analysis and Interpretation**

Name	Formula	Meaning
Profitability		
Gross profit %	$\dfrac{\text{Gross profit}}{\text{Net sales}} \times \dfrac{100}{1}$	Shows the percentage of each sales dollar that is available to meet the expenses of the business and provide a return to the owner.
Markup %	$\dfrac{\text{Gross profit}}{\text{Cost of goods sold}} \times \dfrac{100}{1}$	Shows the percentage added to the cost of goods sold to determine the selling price.
Distribution cost %	$\dfrac{\text{Distribution costs}}{\text{Net sales}} \times \dfrac{100}{1}$	Shows the percentage of each sales dollar that is used to meet distribution costs.
Administrative expense %	$\dfrac{\text{Administrative expenses}}{\text{Net sales}} \times \dfrac{100}{1}$	Shows the percentage of each sales dollar that is used to meet administrative expenses.
Finance cost %	$\dfrac{\text{Finance costs}}{\text{Net sales}} \times \dfrac{100}{1}$	Shows the percentage of each sales dollar that is used to meet finance costs.
Total expense %	$\dfrac{\text{Total expenses}}{\text{Net sales}} \times \dfrac{100}{1}$	Shows the percentage of each sales dollar that is used to meet total expenses.
Profit %	$\dfrac{\text{Profit for the year}}{\text{Net sales}} \times \dfrac{100}{1}$	Shows the percentage of each sales dollar that is available as a return to the owner.
Return on equity %	$\dfrac{\text{Profit for the year}}{\text{Average equity}} \times \dfrac{100}{1}$	Shows the efficiency with which the firm used the owner's capital to generate profit. If adjusted for the value of the owner's work in the business, can be used to compare the return from the business with other forms of investment.
Return on total assets %	$\dfrac{\text{Profit for the year + interest}}{\text{Average total assets}} \times \dfrac{100}{1}$	Shows the efficiency with which the firm used business assets to generate profit, independently of the means of financing. Can be compared with the cost of finance to see if the return generated from assets is worthwhile.

Gross profit and markup percentages have both increased in 2026, which has left an additional 2.6 cents of each sales dollar available to cover expenses. However, the total expense percentage also increased so that an additional 4.8 cents in each sales dollar was used to cover expenses, the most significant increase being in distribution costs. The net result was a *decrease* in the profit percentage from 13.5% to 11.3%, a difference of 2.2 cents per dollar of sales.

While this decrease in the profit *percentage* may appear to be unfavourable, we must remember that sales increased in *dollar* terms, so that the lower percentage is more than compensated by the increase in dollar sales. The profit for the year *increased* by $25,375.

The return on equity and return on total assets percentages have both *increased*. The return on equity calculation has not allowed for any 'salary' to the owner so is not an accurate measure of the real return on capital invested. However, the trend is positive and hence favourable. The return on total assets is extremely favourable because *Energised Electronics* has increased its asset base and at the same time managed to increase the efficiency with which those assets have been employed. The return of 29.6% is well above the 8% cost of finance on

 PHOTOCOPYING PROHIBITED

ISBN: 9780170262415

the long-term loan.

Overall, we must conclude that profitability trends are *favourable*. The expansion of the business largely through the use of debt finance, together with the change of supplier, has resulted in a higher dollar profit figure and more efficient use of assets.

This example illustrates the importance of examining dollar figures from the financial statements alongside the calculated percentages. On their own, the increase in the total expense percentage and the decrease in the profit percentage would appear to be unfavourable. It is only by examining the dollar figures that we were able to draw the correct conclusion.

Management efficiency and financial structure

A summary of measures of management efficiency and financial structure is:

Name	Formula	Meaning
Management efficiency		
Age of accounts receivable (debtors' turnover)	$\dfrac{\text{Average accounts receivable}}{\text{Credit sales + GST}} \times \dfrac{365}{1}$	Shows the average number of days that debtors have taken to pay their accounts.
Age of accounts payable (creditors' turnover)	$\dfrac{\text{Average accounts payable}}{\text{Credit purchases + GST}} \times \dfrac{365}{1}$	Shows the average number of days taken to pay suppliers' accounts.
Inventory turnover	$\dfrac{\text{Cost of goods sold}}{\text{Average inventory}}$	Shows the number of times per annum that the average inventory has been sold = x times per annum. The number of days taken can be found by dividing 365 by x.
Operating cycle	Age of accounts receivable (days) + inventory turnover (days)	Shows the length of time between purchasing goods and collecting cash from credit customers.
Cash cycle	Age of accounts receivable (days) + inventory turnover (days) − accounts payable (days)	Shows the length of time between paying for goods and collecting cash from credit customers.
Liquidity and financial structure		
Working capital	Current assets − current liabilities	Shows the surplus of current assets after current liabilities have been met in the next reporting period.
Current ratio	$\dfrac{\text{Current assets}}{\text{Current liabilities}}$	Shows the amount of current assets available to meet each dollar of current liabilities in the next reporting period.
Liquid capital	Quick assets − quick liabilities	Shows the surplus of cash or equivalents after current liabilities have been paid in the immediate future (next month or so).
Liquid ratio	$\dfrac{\text{Quick assets}}{\text{Quick liabilities}}$ OR $\dfrac{\text{Current assets} - (\text{inventory} + \text{prepayments})}{\text{Current liabilities} - \text{secured bank overdraft}}$	Shows the amount of cash or equivalents available to meet each dollar of current liabilities in the immediate future (next month or so).
Equity ratio	$\dfrac{\text{Equity}}{\text{Total assets}}$	Shows the proportion of business assets financed by the owner.

The table below summarises the measures of management efficiency and financial structure for *Energised Electronics*.

	2025	2026
Age of accounts receivable	8 days	8 days
Inventory turnover	18.0 times	11.4 times
Current ratio	0.70:1	2.34:1
Liquid ratio	0.53:1	0.93:1
Equity ratio	0.56:1	0.47:1

The age of accounts receivable is very *favourable* and has remained steady at 8 days, indicating that control over debtors is efficient. The inventory turnover has slowed down from 18 times per annum (20 days) to 11.4 times (32 days), which is *unfavourable*. At the same time the cost of inventory on hand has trebled.

The current ratio has improved from an unsatisfactory 0.70:1 in 2025 to a satisfactory 2.34:1 in 2026. This means that there is $2.34 available in current assets to meet current liabilities in the next reporting period. Increasing the long-term bank loan to repay the overdraft has improved short-term liquidity. However, the immediate liquidity position is unfavourable, with only 93 cents becoming available to meet liabilities due to be paid in the next month or so. It will be necessary to use the bank overdraft facility to meet these immediate debts.

This immediate liquidity position arises from the large quantity of inventory on hand, most of which has been purchased for cash, leaving the business short of cash for other purposes.

The equity ratio has decreased and is now 0.47:1, which means that 47% of the business assets have been financed by the owner. This is a marginal position that could leave the business at risk from creditors if their accounts are not paid on time. Owner's drawings have increased by only 1%, so have had no significant effect. The main reason for the change in the equity ratio was the increased bank loan raised to finance expansion.

Conclusions and recommendations

Energised Electronics has undergone an expansion programme in 2026 involving:
- the purchase of additional delivery vans
- increasing inventory on hand
- increasing staffing levels.

The expansion has been very successful in improving profitability, with an increase in profit for the year and improvements in the return on equity and return on total assets employed.

At year-end, there is insufficient cash on hand to meet immediate liabilities and it will be necessary to use the bank overdraft facility to pay these. It is recommended that the inventory purchasing policy be reassessed. The following questions should be addressed:
- Is it necessary to hold this high level of inventory on hand to qualify for quantity discounts?
- Is it necessary to pay for inventory in cash or would the supplier consider offering additional credit facilities?

Reducing inventory levels and/or using supplier credit would reduce pressure on cash flow.

The equity ratio is marginal. If possible, owner's drawings should be reduced until the business has retained sufficient profit to reduce the level of debt.

ISBN: 9780170262415

Interrelationships between Analysis Measures

Certain ratios and percentages are related to each other and groups of them must be examined together if an accurate assessment of the business financial performance and position is to be made. Some examples of groups of ratios and percentages which should be examined together are shown in the table below.

Measures	Interrelationship
Gross profit % Expense % Profit %	The gross profit percentage and expense percentages determine the profit percentage. *For example:* • if the gross profit percentage increases but the total expense percentage increases by a greater amount, there will be a fall in the profit percentage; • the profit percentage will increase if there is an increase in the gross profit percentage and expense percentages remain the same; • the profit percentage will increase if the gross profit percentage remains constant but expense percentages fall.
Return on equity % Equity ratio Return on total assets %	Differences between the return on equity and the return on total assets depend on the level of gearing as shown by the equity ratio. *For example:* If the business increases its total assets by borrowing, • the equity ratio will fall; • the return on the total assets percentage will decrease unless the profit increases by the same proportion as the total assets; • the return on equity percentage is not affected by the change in the level of debt; • the lower equity ratio results in a smaller difference between return on equity and return on total assets percentages.
Current ratio Liquid ratio Age of accounts receivable Inventory turnover	Accounts receivable and inventory both tie up business cash and hence affect liquidity. *For example:* • High current and liquid ratios with a long age of accounts receivable may mean that there are bad debts, which are causing accounts receivable to be artificially high and thus both current and liquid ratios are inflated; • High current and liquid ratios with an acceptable age of accounts receivable may mean that the business is holding too much cash and should invest some of this to earn interest; • A high current ratio with a low liquid ratio and slow inventory turnover means that there is too much slow-moving inventory on hand that should be sold at reduced prices to obtain cash; • A satisfactory current ratio with a low liquid ratio and acceptable inventory turnover may mean that the business has used an unsecured bank overdraft to buy property, plant and equipment which should be financed using long-term debt.

Limitations of Ratio Analysis

At best, the ratios and percentages provide a guide as to areas of the business that are satisfactory and those that may require further investigation:

- ratios and percentages that are calculated for a business must be examined in conjunction with the financial statements themselves;
- financial statements are usually prepared on an annual basis, hence may or may not represent the *average* position of the business during the year;
- it is impossible to draw definite conclusions from one year's financial statements – it is the *trends* in ratios and percentages over a number of years that give the best picture of a business;
- comparison with industry averages (ratios and percentages averaged over a number of businesses in the same industry group) is often helpful in assessing the financial performance and position of a business in relation to others.

Activities

1. The information below relates to *Asian Artifacts*, an importer of collectibles and curios, for the year ended 31 March 2026.

Total Assets = $273,600

Cash at bank $38,000	Accounts receivable $69,400	Inventory $16,600	Property, plant and equipment $149,600

Total Liabilities and Equity = $273,600

Current liabilities $20,000	Bank loan (9%) $109,600	Equity $144,000

Income statement summary for the year ended 31 March 2026	
Sales (25% credit)	$1,200,000
Cost of goods sold	760,000
Gross profit	440,000
Distribution costs	140,000
Administrative expenses	180,200
Finance costs	9,800
Total expenses	330,000
Profit for the year	$110,000

Additional information at 31 March 2025	
Accounts receivable	$50,600
Inventory	15,600
Equity	84,000

Industry averages 31 March 2026 Variety Stores	
Age of accounts receivable	30 days
Inventory turnover	26 times
Return on equity %	36.9%

DO THIS!

a Complete the calculations in the table provided.
b Answer the questions that follow.

a Complete the table below.

	2026	Working
Current ratio		
Liquid ratio		
Inventory turnover		
Age of accounts receivable		
Equity ratio		
Return on equity percentage		

The owner of *Asian Artifacts* has been away for the past year and employed a manager to run the business during that time. He is keen to assess the manager's performance in terms of inventory management, age of accounts receivable and cash management.

b **i** Fully explain the meaning of the industry average of 26 days for inventory turnover in 2026.

_____

_____

_____

_____

_____

ii Justify why the inventory turnover of *Asian Artifacts* in 2026 may be considered to be either *favourable* or *unfavourable*.

_____

_____

_____

_____

_____

_____

_____

_____

_____

iii Fully explain the meaning of the industry average of 30 days for age of accounts receivable in 2026.

_____

_____

_____

_____

iv Justify whether the age of accounts receivable of *Asian Artifacts* in 2026 is *favourable* or *unfavourable*.

_____

_____

_____

_____

_____

_____

_____

_____

_____

_____

ISBN: 9780170262415

v Justify whether or not the owner should be concerned about the current and liquid ratios of *Asian Artifacts* in 2026. You should include in your answer:
- a description of the meaning of both current and liquid ratios of *Asian Artifacts*
- a justified explanation of the influence of inventory turnover on the interpretation of the current and liquid ratios
- a justified explanation of the influence of the age of accounts receivable on the interpretation of the current and liquid ratios
- a justified assessment of the liquidity position of *Asian Artifacts*.

_____

_____

_____

_____

_____

_____

_____

_____

_____

_____

_____

_____

_____

_____

_____

_____

_____

_____

_____

_____

_____

_____

_____

_____

_____

_____

_____

_____

_____

ISBN: 9780170262415

ASIAN
RTIFACTS

The owner has examined the profitability and financial structure of *Asian Artifacts* and is considering repaying $20,000 of the bank loan, using cash from the business bank account. However he wishes to ensure that this would not have an unfavourable effect on either the equity ratio or the return on equity percentage.

vi Make a justified recommendation as to whether or not the owner should proceed with repaying the loan. You should include in your answer:

- a description of the meaning of the equity ratio of *Asian Artifacts*
- an explanation of why the owner is concerned about the effect on the equity ratio
- an explanation of the effect of repaying $20,000 on the equity ratio
- a description of the meaning of the return on equity percentage of *Asian Artifacts*
- an explanation of the effect of repaying $20,000 on the return on equity percentage
- an explanation of any risk involved in repaying long-term debt
- a justified recommendation as to whether the $20,000 should be used to repay part of the bank loan or invested at 5% per annum interest in a term deposit.

_____
_____
_____
_____
_____
_____
_____
_____
_____
_____
_____
_____
_____
_____
_____
_____
_____
_____
_____
_____
_____
_____
_____
_____
_____

Additional answer space is available on page 79

2 The information below has been extracted from the financial statements of *Roofrite* for the past two years. The annual reporting period ends on 30 September.

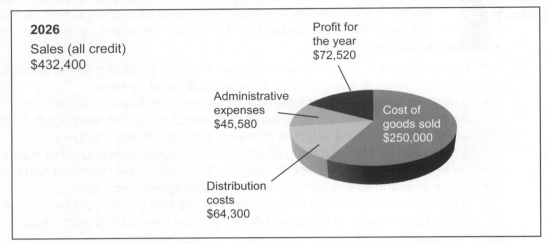

2026

Sales (all credit)
$432,400

Profit for the year $72,520

Administrative expenses $45,580

Distribution costs $64,300

Cost of goods sold $250,000

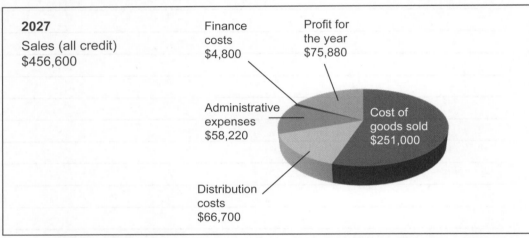

2027

Sales (all credit)
$456,600

Finance costs $4,800

Profit for the year $75,880

Administrative expenses $58,220

Distribution costs $66,700

Cost of goods sold $251,000

Statements of Financial Position (summary) as at 30 September		
	2026 $	2027 $
Assets		
Current assets		
Cash at bank	2,900	—
Accounts receivable	26,280	27,840
Inventory	17,200	14,800
Prepayments	620	360
	47,000	43,000
Non-current assets		
Property, plant and equipment	32,840	70,920
Goodwill	10,000	30,000
Total assets	**$89,840**	**$143,920**
Liabilities		
Current liabilities		
Bank overdraft	—	9,120
Accounts payable	28,200	23,120
GST payable	5,600	4,400
Accrued expenses	1,000	360
	34,800	37,000
Non-current liabilities		
Bank loan	—	40,000
Total liabilities	**$34,800**	**$77,000**

 PHOTOCOPYING PROHIBITED

ISBN: 9780170262415

Statements of Financial Position (summary) as at 30 September		
	2026 $	2027 $
Equity		
Opening capital	62,520	55,040
Profit for the year	72,520	75,880
Drawings	(80,000)	(64,000)
Closing capital	**$55,040**	**$66,920**

Income Statement Analysis Measures for the years ended 30 September		
	2026	2027
Gross profit %	42.2%	45.0%
Distribution cost %	14.9%	14.6%
Administrative expense %	10.5%	12.8%
Finance cost %	0.0%	1.1%
Profit for the year %	16.8%	16.5%

October 2026

14 Wednesday
Check that $40,000 bank loan has been deposited in bank account

October 2026

19 Monday
Settlement day for purchase of Ready Roofing

December 2026

17 Thursday
Arrange $10,000 overdraft secured against equipment

DO THIS!

a Complete the calculations in the table provided.
b Answer the questions that follow.

a Complete the table below and on the next page.

	2026	2027	Working
Current ratio	1.35:1		
Liquid ratio	0.84:1		
Inventory turnover	15.2 times		
Age of accounts receivable	19 days		

	2026	2027	Working
Equity ratio	0.61:1		
Return on equity percentage	123.4%		
Return on total assets percentage	78.1%		

b **i** Explain the reasons for the trend in the finance cost percentage.

_____

_____

_____

_____

_____

_____

_____

ii Explain whether or not the owner of *Roofrite* should be concerned about the trend in the finance cost percentage and why.

_____

_____

_____

_____

_____

_____

_____

iii Explain the reasons for the trend in the profit for the year percentage and present a justified opinion as to whether it is significant or not.

_____

_____

_____

_____

_____

_____

_____

_____

_____

_____

_____

_____

_____

ISBN: 9780170262415

_____

_____

_____

_____

_____

_____

iv Explain whether or not the owner of *Roofrite* should be concerned about the liquidity of the business and why. You should include in your answer:
- a description of the trends in the current and liquid ratios of *Roofrite*
- an explanation of the meanings of the 2027 ratios
- an explanation of the meaning of the age of accounts receivable and its importance in assessing liquidity
- a justified explanation of the reasons for the trends and an assessment of liquidity at 30 September 2027
- a justified recommendation as to how the liquidity position could be improved in future.

_____

_____

_____

_____

_____

_____

_____

_____

_____

_____

_____

_____

_____

_____

_____

_____

_____

_____

_____

_____

_____

_____

_____

continued on next page

ISBN: 9780170262415

 PHOTOCOPYING PROHIBITED

Analysis and Interpretation

_____
_____
_____
_____
_____
_____
_____
_____
_____
_____
_____

v Explain whether or not the owner of *Roofrite* should be concerned about the financial structure of the business and why. You should include in your answer:
- an explanation of the meaning of the 2026 and 2027 equity ratios of *Roofrite* and an explanation of the reasons for the trend
- a justified assessment of financial structure at 30 September 2027, including an explanation of any current risk
- a justified recommendation as to how the financial structure could be improved in future.

_____
_____
_____
_____
_____
_____
_____
_____
_____
_____
_____
_____
_____
_____
_____
_____
_____
_____
_____
_____
_____
_____

ISBN: 9780170262415

SPARE ANSWER SPACE

_____
_____
_____
_____
_____
_____
_____
_____
_____
_____
_____
_____
_____
_____
_____
_____
_____
_____
_____
_____
_____
_____
_____
_____
_____
_____
_____
_____
_____
_____
_____
_____
_____
_____
_____
_____

ISBN: 9780170262415

 PHOTOCOPYING PROHIBITED

Analysis and Interpretation

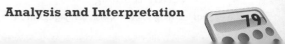

Index

NCEA – Accounting a Next Step – Level Two is a new series of combined textbook/workbooks which has been specifically designed to meet the requirements of the revised Level 2 Achievement Standards in accounting.

Analysis and Interpretation is a stand-alone textbook/workbook that has been designed specifically to cover Achievement Standard 91177 (2.4).

Following the popular format of the *Senior Accounting* series, this volume contains fully explained text with comprehensive worked examples, interspersed with graduated activities that develop students' skills and confidence as the topic progresses.

Solutions to all of the exercises are provided in the *Teachers' Guide*, which is an overprinted version of the student edition that provides a quick reference for teachers. This format has proved to be particularly useful in catering for a class where students are working at their own pace. An electronic copy of the *Teachers' Guide* is included for use as visual media.

The Authors

Lilian Viitakangas is an educational consultant. She was a Senior Tutor at The University of Auckland, where she specialised in teacher education and the teaching of introductory accounting courses. Formerly HOD Business Studies at Glenfield College, Lilian has more than twenty years' teaching experience spanning secondary, tertiary and adult education both in New Zealand and overseas. Lilian is a former examiner for University Entrance, Bursaries and Scholarships, the New Zealand Education and Scholarship Trust and the Sixth Form External Examination in accounting.

Alastair Campbell is Specialist Classroom Teacher and HOD Business Studies at Macleans College. He has an extensive business background in accounting, sales and marketing and is an experienced marker of external accounting examinations at various levels.

CHECK OUT OUR WEBSITE!

Follow the link www.nelsonsecondary.co.nz/nceaaccountinglevel2 to find some useful resources. A full glossary is available in both English and Chinese and other resources will be added from time to time.

NELSON
CENGAGE Learning
For learning solutions, visit cengage.com.au

ISBN: 978-0170262415
9 780170 262415